ALTERNATIVES TO DOMESTIC VIOLENCE

ALTERNATIVES TO
DOMESTIC VIOLENCE

A Homework Manual for
Battering Intervention Groups

Kevin A. Fall, Ph.D.
Assistant Professor
Loyola University of New Orleans

Shareen Howard, M.S.
Director of the Battering Intervention
and Prevention Program
Denton County Friends of the Family

June E. Ford, LMSW, M.S.S.W.
Executive Director
Carriage House Assisted Living

USA	Publishing Office:	Accelerated Development
		A member of the Taylor & Francis Group
		325 Chestnut Street
		Philadelphia, PA 19106
		Tel: (215) 625-8900
		Fax: (215) 625-2940
	Distribution Center:	Accelerated Development
		A member of the Taylor & Francis Group
		47 Runway Road, Suite G
		Levittown, PA 19057-4700
		Tel: (215) 269-0400
		Fax: (215) 269-0363
UK		Accelerated Development
		A member of the Taylor & Francis Group
		1 Gunpowder Square
		London EC4A 3DE
		Tel: +44 171 583 0490
		Fax: +44 171 583 0581

ALTERNATIVES TO DOMESTIC VIOLENCE: A Homework Manual for Battering Intervention Groups

1 2 3 4 5 6 7 8 9 0

Printed by Edwards Brothers, Ann Arbor, MI, 1999.
Cover design by Joan Wendt.

A CIP catalog record for this book is available from the British Library.

∞ The paper in this publication meets the requirements of the ANSI Standard Z39.48-1984 (Permanence of Paper).

Library of Congress Cataloging-in-Publication Data
    Fall, Kevin A.
      Alternatives to domestic violence : a homework manual for battering
intervention groups / Kevin A. Fall, Shareen Howard, June Ford.
        p.   cm.
    Includes bibliographical references.
    ISBN 1-56032-743-X (pbk. : alk. paper)
      1. Family violence—United States—Prevention.   2. Conjugal violence—
United States—Prevention.   3. Abusive men—United States—Psychology.
    4. Abusive men—rehabilitation—United States.
    I. Howard, Shareen. II. Ford, June. III. Title.
    HV6626.2.F34   1999
    362.82'927'0973—dc21   98-37506
                                                                 CIP

1-56032-743-X

TABLE OF CONTENTS

ACKNOWLEDGMENTS

We would like to acknowledge with our thanks some of the individuals who made this book possible. We thank Denton County Friends of the Family, the agency and all the staff, for their help, patience, support, and sound advice. Deborah Cosimo, in particular, provided us with the wisdom and passion to work with this social issue, and she continues to be a mentor, guide, and friend.

We would like to thank all of our group members who have had the courage to be accountable for their abusive thoughts and behaviors and who have taken the time and effort to change. It is through your change that we are all inspired. We recognize and write this book for the survivors of domestic violence and all those who are continuing to suffer in silence.

K. A. F., S. H., and J. E. F.

PREFACE

INTRODUCTION FOR GROUP LEADERS

If you are a mental health professional working with battering intervention groups, then you are keenly aware of the interesting mix of frustration and exhilaration that these groups can produce. In all our experiences with groups, it would be difficult to find another population with such interesting dynamics: angry, ashamed, responsible, irresponsible, street-smart, book-smart, scared, intimidating, confused, mean, poor, rich, old, young—the list could go on and on and it still would not encompass the diversity in any one battering intervention group.

In facilitating groups for this population, many group leaders follow a curriculum that has been well researched and published. The curriculum in which we and many others have been trained and use is the Duluth model (Pence & Paymar, 1993). Regardless of which curriculum is followed, each provides a common language and a set of common rules for treatment. It also provides an empirical base and rationale for conceptualization, treatment, and further research.

We developed this book, not because we were dissatisfied with the existing programs, but because the programs themselves allowed for creative expansion. As we worked with the groups, we began to experiment with different techniques or expand on existing techniques to improve the quality of the group experience. This book is the product of that experimentation and refinement. The topics have been kept similar to most battering program curriculums so integration would be smooth. Exercises in Chapters 2 through 6—*Achieving Nonviolence, Exploring and Defeating Intimidation, Creating a Trusting Relationship, Giving and Receiving Respect,* and *Accountability: Taking Responsibility for Yourself*—all will give you a chance to broaden the client's learning within your program's individual approach. Chapter 6, *Accountability: Taking Responsibility for Yourself,* has been given a lot of attention because it probably is the most important concept in the process of change. These exercises provide the unique blend of exploration and direct confrontation that has been successful in our own groups.

We believe the remaining chapters are an immense improvement on the existing program approaches. In Chapter 7, *Maintaining Positive Sexual Relationships,* exercises are designed to hit at the core of the male experience and help facilitate change within this topic. These exercises target universal male issues such as sexual myths, intimacy and pornography. One exercise explores rape and is active and forceful in challenging men to work to end rape in our society.

Chapter 8, *Negotiating a Partnership*, covers the basic ideas of an equal relationship, but also takes a comprehensive look at using finances as a means of negotiating partnership. In facilitating our battering groups, we were struck by the frequency with which the men used money to control and gain an upper hand in relationships. Developing exercises that helped group members explore their beliefs and actions in the area of money has proven to be very valuable. Chapter 9, *Cooperating Through Good Communication*, also covers a very basic skill in a way that encourages change in the group members. As one group member stated after completing the chapter, "I had no idea there was such value in listening."

Parenting: How to Relate to Your Children, Chapter 10, is vital and provides an excellent addition to any program. Many men in groups do not realize the impact of violence on their children. Using this impact can be an impetus to change for many of the members. The exercises also give them an opportunity to learn key skills in being a noncontrolling parent as they attempt to learn to be a noncontrolling partner. The final exercise on balancing work and family has been invaluable and always sparks an emotional response within the group.

Each exercise was cultivated through direct use with battering groups. We have created and tried out many exercises that have met with differing success from the point of view of both facilitator and member. The exercises that were chosen for the book are ones that seemed to produce quality experiences in group after group. By quality experiences, we mean a variety of actions such as consistently completed homework by everyone in the group, a spirited group discussion, self-disclosure by a group member, and almost any occurrence which takes the group to a deeper level of understanding. Along these lines, just as each exercise is imbued with the life of group experiences, some of the exercises use actual stories from actual group members. Although their names have been changed to protect their confidentiality, their stories will strike a universal chord with your group members. As we all know, it is easier for a group to hear something from another member of the group than it is to hear it from the leader.

We know that the vast majority of battering is male-to-female. The thrust of the book is looking at male battering, but we recognize that the field is taking a look at the violence of women and the idea of mutual combat. Many of these exercises can be used for any population if the goal is to reduce domestic violence.

The key to this book is that it is a *homework* book. We believe, because a group meeting is only approximately two hours long, that the majority of the change and learning is going to occur outside of the group. Having an instrument to provide an outlet for learning outside the group can be the bridge that some group members need to make a change. Although most curricula have homework assignments, they are often repetitive and very structured. We have found, although the educational levels of group members is varied, that they all make a serious attempt to complete the homework. Each exercise is designed to be brought back to the group for discussion.

We encourage you to use this book as a homework tool for your groups by having each member purchase one at the beginning of the group. The price has been kept low to make the book an affordable option. We have found that the members who pay for the book take more responsibility in their homework and in their change process in general. The book, in itself, becomes an accountability instrument and, therefore, an agent of change.

We appreciate the work you are doing with this population and wish you the best of luck in your groups.

Kevin A. Fall
Shareen Howard
June E. Ford
May 1, 1998

INTRODUCTION FOR GROUP MEMBERS

If you are reading this section, then you have picked up this book in one of two ways. Either you are an individual who is concerned about some aspect of abuse in your life or you are a member of a battering intervention group who has been encouraged to buy this book as a part of your counseling. In either case, you are in the right place so let us welcome you to a process that will be both challenging and rewarding.

This book is designed to be an "add-on" to what you do in group. If you aren't in a group yet, let us strongly encourage you to join one in your area. If you are concerned about your behavior, or if someone you know has voiced their concern, it is in your best interest to try to change before the abuse destroys your life. The change process is a hard one and is largely determined by how much effort you are willing to put into the process. The exercises in this book were created to help you continue the learning process outside of your group time.

You need to know that group members—men like you—made a large contribution to this book. This book was not created in some laboratory in a far away land. It was built using groups and the opinions and ideas of individuals just like yourself. The stories you read in this book are from actual group members, although their names have been changed to protect their confidentiality. You will experience how people like you have taken the challenge to change. Some have found success, others have failed. Through these exercises you will have an opportunity to learn from both.

As we mentioned earlier, the main reason we wrote this book was because the time we spent in group was not enough. The time you spend in group is not enough to promote a change. You have to practice and be challenged all week long. We also believe that you, as an individual who wants to change, must work the program with intense effort. In the beginning, you may believe that you do not need to change. That is fine, but you owe it to yourself, your children, and your partner to get as much out of this process as you can. At the very least, you paid for it so get your money's worth!

One thing we always tell our new group members is that the information that you receive in this book is like various tools in a toolbox. In your present life you have tools in your toolbox. Each tool represents a strategy for handling certain problems. For most people starting this process, violence, abuse and control are tools that they have relied on and have used in their lives. The exercises in this book are just new tools to add to your toolbox. Some you may find useful, others will only be used for specialized occasions, while others you will never choose to use in any situation. But one thing we have learned is that it is not our job, nor within our ability, to make you choose the new tools. You have to choose them on your own.

Well, enough reading. It is time to get to work. Choose your tools wisely and good luck!

Kevin A. Fall
Shareen Howard
June Ford
May 1, 1998

Chapter 1

DEFINING ABUSE AND BATTERING

I n order to set the tone for the book, it is necessary for the readers and authors to come to some agreement on the definitions of key terms used throughout this workbook. The following exercises will help you explore the various meanings of words and concepts that will be vital to the change process. It is highly recommended that you complete the defining exercises with as much detail as possible in order to get the most out of the remaining chapters.

1. Define "abuse." Give examples of some actions that you consider abusive._____

   _____

   _____

   _____

   _____

2. Define "battering." Give examples of behaviors you believe are battering behaviors._____

   _____

   _____

   _____

   _____

Exercise 1.1
Defining Abuse and Battering

Bobby's Story

Read the following story of one man who was interviewed for this book. After reading his story, use the information to answer the questions concerning the definition of abuse and battering.

I don't understand what went wrong. Lisa and I were a happy couple for the first year, then everything changed. First, she had a baby and that really put a lot of stress on me. She started being too tired to do anything with me. She wanted to get a job because she said we didn't have enough money. I considered that an insult. I mean, my job is making the money and she needs to take care of my son. I had the phone turned off because she was spending so much money talking to her mother! She didn't like that, but she was the one who was complaining about money. I started going out more with my friends and I would drink, but not too much really. She was always on me about going out and drinking. Hey, I make the money, I should be able to go out once in awhile.

She complained so much! It would usually end with us getting into an argument. I would yell, call her a "moron" or a "whore." She would start crying. If she kept nagging me I would threaten to leave her. She usually shut up after that.

Anyway, one night I came home and she started in on me. I just couldn't take it. I lost control and threw a shoe at her. When she tried to leave with the kid, I stood in her way and grabbed the keys. She still tried to leave, so I pushed her down on the couch. I told her "Don't think about leaving. You won't make it out the door."

I didn't mean anything by it, but she got scared and called the police. She's so weak. She knows I get angry and she doesn't seem to realize that it's my way or the highway now. Now I'm better. I would never touch her. When I get mad, I just punch the wall or door to let her know I'm angry. That seems to do the trick. She calms down and I calm down.

EXERCISE 1.1: BOBBY'S STORY

Processing Questions

1. Go through Bobby's Story and circle behaviors or attitudes that you consider abusive.

2. Go through Bobby's story and underline behaviors or attitudes that you consider to be battering.

3. Based on the story, how did your definition of "abuse" change? Write your new definition below._____

   _____

   _____

   _____

   _____

4. Based on the story, how did your definition of "battering" change? Write your new definition below._____

   _____

   _____

   _____

   _____

5. Based on your definition of "abuse" and "battering," discuss some of your behaviors (both past and present) that fit either of these definitions._____

   _____

   _____

   _____

   _____

   _____

FOUR FORMS OF ABUSE

At this point, you have had the opportunity to explore some important words in battering intervention: "abuse" and "battering." They are important because how we define them will determine the steps we take to overcome the problem. In the authors' experience, individuals in the beginning stage of the change process often have a limited view of the true scope of the problem. To make sure that the reader know the authors' definition of the terms, "abuse" and "battering" will each be defined.

In this book, abuse is any attitude or behavior that results in harming another individual. Harm is usually inflicted in predominantly four ways: physically, verbally, emotionally, or sexually.

Physical Abuse

Physical abuse is often the most recognized form of abuse. Actual contact between two people is noticeable by the red marks, bruises, scratches, and broken bones. This form of abuse is destructive physically and emotionally to the victim of the attack. In most cases, when reported, this form of abuse has legal consequences. The following list provides some examples of physical abuse by contact:

- Pushing
- Grabbing
- Pulling hair

- Punching
- Slapping
- Kicking

- Spanking
- Restraining
- Choking

Although physical abuse by contact is readily recognized, physical abuse also can be found in other forms. Intimidation is physical abuse without touching another person. Often, men will use their physical size and strength to intimidate a partner. In Bobby's story, Bobby stood in the doorway and refused to let Lisa leave the house. This blocking behavior is abusive because it controls Lisa's behavior and freedom of choice. Often, men are unaware of how their size intimidates others. Some exercises in the following chapters will allow you to explore this possibility. Some examples of intimidation as physical abuse are:

- Blocking someone's path

- Getting in someone's face

- Taking objects away from someone

- Flexing muscles, clenching fists

Objects can also be used to abuse another person physically. In Bobby's story, Bobby reported feeling good about hitting the wall when he got angry. Although many would agree that hitting the wall is a better alternative to hitting Lisa, the action of hitting the wall is still abusive because of the fear it causes in Lisa. Exercises in the next chapter will aid your understanding of the role of fear and behaviors such as hitting walls and tables. The following are examples of the use of objects as physical abuse:

- Throwing objects

- Breaking objects

- Slamming doors

- Driving dangerously

- Destroying someone else's personal property

Verbal Abuse

Verbal abuse is the use of words or tone of voice to control or harm another person. The impact of verbal abuse on its victims is most often feelings of fear, hopelessness, guilt, and pain. In Bobby's story, Bobby called Lisa names such as "moron" and "whore." The names picked tell us something about how Bobby views Lisa. Bobby wants Lisa to feel stupid and worthless, so he chooses words to send that message. Bobby also uses threats of physical violence and abandonment to control Lisa. Threats act as a verbal paralyzing technique, designed to control and freeze another person. The following are some examples of verbal abuse:

- Calling someone names
- Other insults

- Sarcasm
- Accusing

- Blaming
- Threatening

Emotional Abuse

Any of the forms of abuse can be emotionally painful, however, some methods of abuse are directed at harming the person's feelings or sense of self and reality. Tactics of emotional abuse are designed to take the focus off of the batterer and to make the victim take the blame for the problems and to distrust his or her view of reality within the relationship. Bobby made Lisa feel the money issue was her problem by prohibiting Lisa from getting a job, becoming insulted at the idea and turning off the phone so she couldn't talk to her family. Bobby insisted the money problem was solved by curbing Lisa's spending. Refocusing the issue and isolation are common forms of emotional abuse. Bobby also goes out drinking with his friends and does not see this as a problem. Going out with friends is not abusive by itself, but ignoring Lisa's concerns about the situation is abusive because Bobby is refusing to take Lisa's concerns seriously. The following are more examples of emotional abuse:

- Insulting another's friends

- Being critical of ideas

- Having affairs

- Isolating your partner from family or friends

- Drinking/doing drugs

- Going through another's personal belongings

- Following/stalking

Sexual Abuse

Sexual abuse involves the control of the sexual relationship to fulfill the batterer's need for control. Controlling sexual attitudes and values can have a destructive impact that is often overlooked in battering relationships. The following represent some examples of sexual abuse:

- Forcing sex (rape)

- Refusing to use birth control

- Forcing fantasies

- Having affairs

- Becoming angry and demanding when denied sex

As you can see, the definition of abuse is much more than a one-time incident of physical contact. Across the areas of physical, verbal, emotional, and sexual abuse, abuse is defined as a process of behaviors designed to control and harm another person (your partner). Throughout this workbook, you will have the opportunity to complete exercises designed to help you become aware of the abusive behaviors and attitudes in your life and work on ways to change the abusive behaviors into cooperative, and noncontrolling actions and attitudes.

Using the definition of abuse, we can broaden the definition of battering. Although, traditionally, battering has been defined by legal terms such as "assault" and "bodily harm," we see battering, like abuse, as a set of attitudes and behaviors designed to control another person. Many individuals do not see themselves as "batterers" even if they repeatedly verbally and emotionally abuse their partners. No matter how you define yourself, participating in these workbook activities will help you move beyond labels and work on changing your controlling attitudes and behaviors. We urge you to keep your expanded definitions of abuse and battering in mind as you work through the rest of the workbook.

Chapter **2**

ACHIEVING NONVIOLENCE

In this chapter, you will have the opportunity to take a look at your experience with violence. Exercises are included to focus specifically on your beliefs and behaviors that are considered violent, abusive, and controlling. If you have been arrested for domestic violence, you are already aware of how the courts define violence. As you discovered in Chapter 1, we believe that the definition of violence and abuse can be expanded to include a wide range of attitudes and actions.

While completing exercises in this chapter, many group members have reported feeling defensive and, at times, ashamed and guilty. The defensiveness may stem from the feeling that the group leaders and society are targeting you as a "bad guy." The fact is that violence and abuse are inappropriate ways of dealing with others. As one group member put it, "I had to finally realize that there was no excuse for my controlling behaviors. If I want everyone out of my business, I have to clean up my act." Although it is not the intention of the exercise to blame or shame you, if those feelings do come up, you are encouraged to explore them, write about them, and discuss them with your group members.

Coming to grips with your violence can be the gateway to understanding some of the more complex issues we will discuss as we use this book. You are encouraged to revisit this chapter as often as you need to do so throughout your change process. The Continuum of Controlling Behaviors exercise is one that we do in group at least once every one to two months. It provides a good personalized refresher for the steps everyone takes when using control on a partner. We wish that reports in the media about abuse were so rare that the Article Homework Assignment could only be completed once. Unfortunately, enough cases of domestic violence occur in some areas that this exercise could be completed every week.

Exercise 2.1
Achieving Nonviolence

The Continuum of Controlling Behaviors

Purpose: In the continuum of male controls over women, Bathrick, Carlin, Kaufman, and Vodde (1987) outline the extensive continuum of control in order to give men insight into the extent of harmful male dominance over women. The Continuum of Controlling Behaviors is an exercise to demonstrate concisely the dynamics of controlling behaviors in a way that can be individualized to each person. This exercise is designed to help you pinpoint your individually chosen controlling behaviors and to understand the dynamics of why controlling behaviors intensify over the course of an argument. Once you can be accountable for your own repertoire of controlling behaviors, attempts can be made to eradicate the controlling behaviors and add non-controlling alternatives to your way of life.

Materials: Tyrone's Story and Tyrone's Continuum.

Procedure: First, read Tyrone's Story. Then, use Tyrone's Continuum as an example for the steps in the continuum process described below.

Step 1. This exercise can be done for any incident in your life. The starting point on the diagram is marked with a small circle. Although many people believe controlling behavior happens without thinking, this model shows that *before* you act, you actually feel and think. This period in time is shown on the diagram as the wavy line between the two circles. When something in our environment poses a problem we always have a moment to think and choose, but we must pay attention to:

1. *Physical cues:* sensations produced in our body that tell us we are angry. These physical cues are different for each individual, so it is important to get a sense for your own cues. For example, Tyrone listed a "racing pulse, clenched fists and a feeling that veins pop up on my head" as his physical cues of anger.

2. *Situational cues:* these are universal "problem areas" in a relationship. Situational cues are best described as topics where a difference of opinion is highly likely (e.g., child discipline, finances, etc.). Tyrone, when completing his continuum after his incident, noticed that "responsibility for housework" is a situational cue for him. This does not mean Tyrone should avoid this topic, but instead, he can pay closer attention to his responses when discussing this topic and be alert for controlling behaviors.

Paying attention to one's physical and emotional cues can help prevent an escalation into controlling behaviors. Unfortunately, most people are not skilled at paying attention to their cues and therefore begin the escalation of controlling behaviors which begins step 2.

Step 2. From the second circle (Figure 2.1), you will notice a long line at about a 45 degree angle. This line represents the continuum of controlling behaviors. Each line represents a controlling behavior, and the intensity of the behaviors will increase going up the continuum. In reviewing Tyrone's story and continuum, as well as your own experience, you will realize that violent behavior does not erupt "out of the blue." There are a series of behaviors that build on one another. Tyrone's incident began with a "look" when he came home and eventually escalated to punching his partner. Everyone has his or her own continuum, and yours may look very similar to or very different from Tyrone's.

Step 3. Notice that there is a line cutting the continuum into two pieces. The actions below the line have two main groupings of characteristics: (1) They are low in intensity and high in frequency, and (2) They have low legal consequences and high relationship consequences. Items that appear on the lower half of the continuum occur frequently in arguments and although they have no legal consequences, they are still destructive to the relationship. The items above the line also have two main groupings of characteristics:

1. They are high in intensity and low in frequency.

2. They have high legal and social consequences.

Step 4. Why do behaviors above the line occur less frequently than the behaviors below the line? Some may say that the legal consequences may keep people from the acting out the behaviors listed above the line. However, the real answer is that the fear of the more intense behaviors makes the lower intensity behaviors work. The fact that batterers have a fear of a violent act recurring is important for two reasons:

1. A one-time act of violence can have long-term relationship consequences due to the fear the batterer's actions created.

2. The lower intensity behaviors become just as intimidating because they are given the power of the more intense behaviors due to the pattern of increasing intensity.

When the batterer gets what he or she wants, the continuum tapers off and escalation ceases. The victim, fearing the more intense response, often gives in earlier in the continuum to avoid physical or sexual consequences. This has a powerful message for the person who uses the line, "I only hit her once" to justify and minimize the impact of the violence. The point that this model demonstrates is that "it" (a high-intensity action) only needs to happen once to set up a system of fear and intimidation. Closely examine Tyrone's continuum and then complete the next exercise in the book.

Note: Killing is placed at the top of the continuum because it is the ultimate form of control. You will get a chance to learn more about this unfortunate, frequent occurrence in Exercise # 4.

EXERCISE 2.1: THE CONTINUUM OF CONTROLLING BEHAVIORS

Tyrone's Story

I will never forget that night. I admit I was mad all day. The boss was on my back and nothing was working out right. On my way home, I could feel my anger inside. My pulse was racing and I could feel the little vein in my head popping out.

When I opened the door to the house, I already knew what to expect. The carpet hadn't been vacuumed, and the kids were running around like they were crazy or something. Jeannie walked in and I gave her this hard, cold stare. She just rolled her eyes and walked into the kitchen. I threw my coat down and the kids went running into their rooms. I guess they smelled trouble. Anyway, I walked in the kitchen and said, "What's with the house?" She said she had been busy all day and didn't get to the floors.

I started yelling and she just kept arguing so I called her a "stupid bitch" and "a worthless mother." She started crying and I walked out. When I came back about 30 minutes later she was still sitting there! I told her to quit whining, that it was no big deal. She started to walk away and I got in her way. She said if I didn't move away, she was going to take the kids and leave. I let go and stood in the doorway and said, "You'll have to get through me first. I swear I'll beat your ass if you try."

She tried to walk by and I grabbed her arm. She tried to wiggle away, but she's pretty weak. I got tired of holding her and listening to her yell at me so I pushed her on the floor. She got up and threw her shoe at me. That really pissed me off. I mean, she had no right hitting me. I charged at her and tried to restrain her. When she tried to scratch me, I punched her in the stomach. She fell to the floor. I think I knocked the wind out of her. Anyway, I guess she came to her senses because she cried for about ten minutes and then said she would vacuum the floors and then make supper.

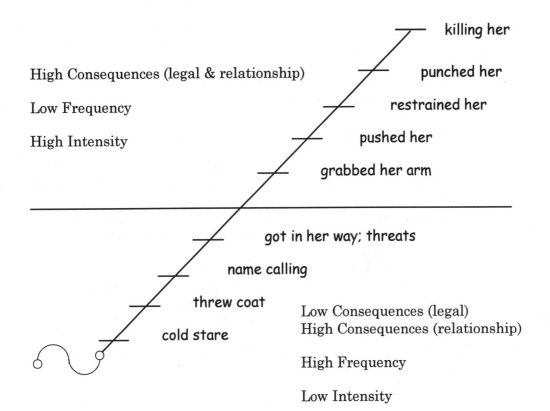

killing her

High Consequences (legal & relationship)

punched her

Low Frequency

restrained her

High Intensity

pushed her

grabbed her arm

got in her way; threats

name calling

threw coat

Low Consequences (legal)
High Consequences (relationship)

cold stare

High Frequency

Low Intensity

Physical Cues:

Racing pulse, clenched fists, vein popping

Situational Cues:

Responsibility for housework

Figure 2.1. Tyrone's Continuum

Exercise 2.2
Achieving Nonviolence

The Personal Continuum of Controlling Behaviors

Purpose: Many times in group, members have said they did not know when they were becoming angry, controlling, or abusive. They often reported a difficulty in identifying their personal signals when becoming angry. They've said comments such as, "I lost it," "my buttons were pushed," "I go from 0-100 in a split second." There are normal ups and downs in a day and in relationships, but there are usually triggers that set up actions which result in "crossing the line" from legal to illegal behaviors. We also know that violent behaviors will increase in intensity if individuals don't take steps to replace their controlling behaviors with non-controlling alternatives. By identifying what is happening to you physically and emotionally, and identifying the situations that seems to generate the most problems for you, you can stop the anger before it gets too far and there are possible legal consequences for your actions. Through the identification process, you can learn new ways of behaving, thinking and feeling so you can move toward non-controlling behaviors and away from controlling behaviors.

Materials: Blank *Continuum of Controlling Behaviors* worksheets.

Procedure: Following the procedure described in the previous exercise, you can construct your own continuum of controlling behaviors using any incident in your life. When completing your continuum, be as specific as possible and discuss your work in group. It will also be helpful to answer the process questions after each time you complete a continuum.

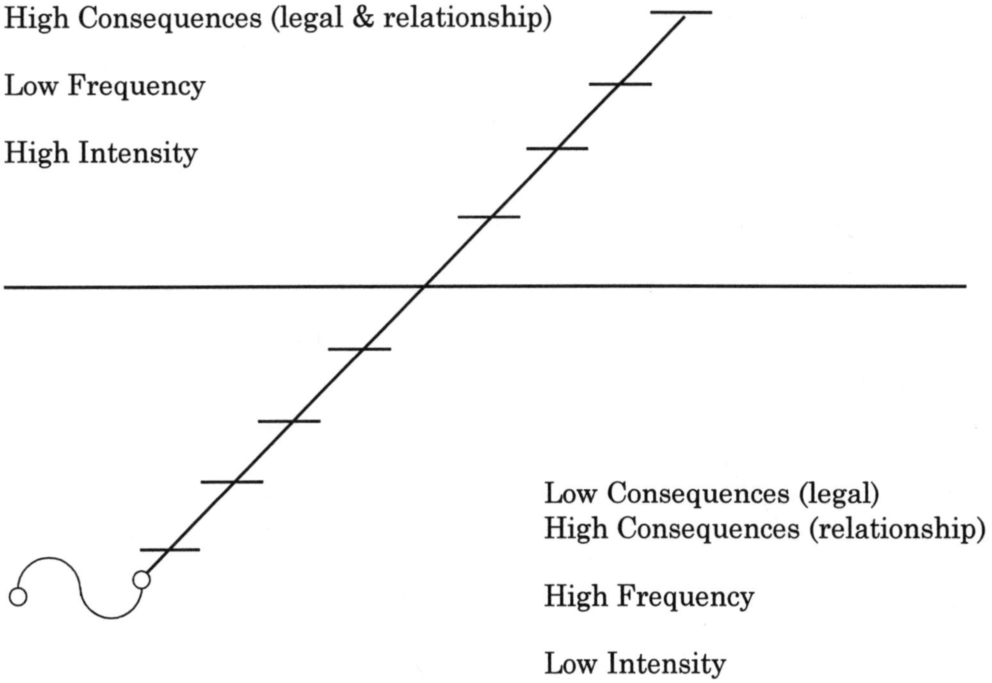

High Consequences (legal & relationship)

Low Frequency

High Intensity

Low Consequences (legal)
High Consequences (relationship)

High Frequency

Low Intensity

Physical Cues:

Situational Cues:

Figure 2.2. Personal Continuum

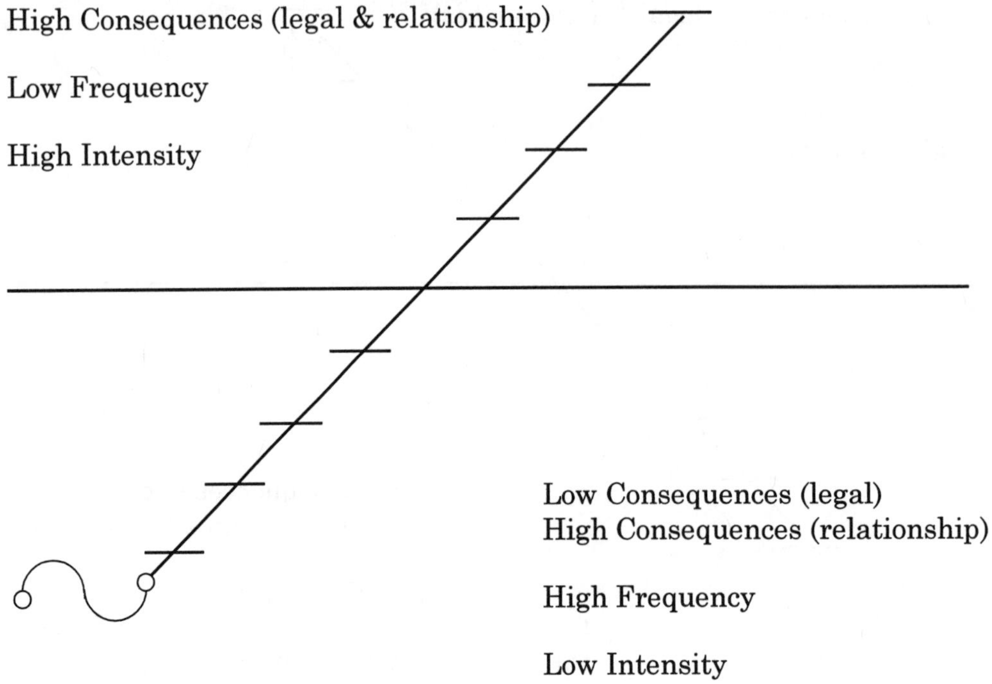

High Consequences (legal & relationship)

Low Frequency

High Intensity

Low Consequences (legal)
High Consequences (relationship)

High Frequency

Low Intensity

Physical Cues:

Situational Cues:

Figure 2.3. Personal Continuum

EXERCISE 2.2: THE PERSONAL
CONTINUUM OF CONTROLLING BEHAVIORS

Process Questions

1. What were you able to learn about your physical signals? List them.

   _____

   _____

   _____

   _____

2. What were you able to learn about your emotional signs? List them.

   _____

   _____

   _____

   _____

3. Were you able to identify situations which frequently result in arguments? List them._____

   _____

   _____

   _____

4. Identify legal and relationship consequences of behaviors below and above the line._____

   _____

   _____

   _____

5. Identify frequency and intensity of behaviors below and above the line. _____

   _____

   _____

   _____

6. Brainstorm ideas for possible nonviolent or non-controlling alternatives to your behavior._____

_____

_____

_____

_____

7. Identify who is/was responsible for de-escalating the continuum?

_____

_____

_____

_____

8. Explore how choosing non-controlling behavior enables you to be more accountable for your own behavior instead of forcing someone else to take responsibility for your "cool down."_____

_____

_____

_____

_____

9. Because fear is the fuel that runs the continuum, discuss how your behaviors promote fear in your partner. What are some signs of that fear?_____

_____

_____

_____

_____

Exercise 2.3
Achieving Nonviolence

Common Bonds of the Experience of Violence

Purpose: Many men have learned that violence is an acceptable and useful way to behave and solve problems. Although it is not an excuse for being abusive, many men have experienced violence, either from peers or their family of origin. The purpose of this exercise is to look at your experiences of violence in your life, whether it is from societal expectations or your family of origin. Each one of you has a personal experience with violence, and many of these are probably common ones you share with other members in your group. A purpose of this exercise is to demonstrate the commonality of your experiences and that you are not alone in your struggle of dealing with violence. In sharing these common experiences, you may become aware of how feelings are allowed (or not allowed) to be expressed by men growing up and see how this is used as an obstacle to not being abusive in a relationship. In particular, becoming aware of how you use abuse to enforce your control over your partner in order to cover up feelings is a necessary step toward change. As you process this with your group, notice not only how the experiences of a child can carry over to the adult life, but also how many people can have similar experiences with violence, but make different choices about using violence in their relationships.

Materials: Experience of Violence Worksheet.

Procedure: Using the Experience of Violence Worksheet, answer yes or no to each item listed. Be as honest as possible, and notice answers that embarrass or concern you. Bring your worksheet to group and discuss your answers with other members. Once you have finished group discussion, answer the process questions on the following page.

EXERCISE 2.3: EXPERIENCE OF VIOLENCE WORKSHEET

Have you ever . . .   Yes   No

1. been in a physical fight as a child?   _____   _____

2. been in a physical fight as an adult?   _____   _____

3. been hit by your mother?   _____   _____

4. been hit by your father?   _____   _____

5. been hit by an older brother or sister?   _____   _____

6. seen someone you respected hit someone they
   "loved"?   _____   _____

7. seen someone you respected get hit by someone
   they "loved"?   _____   _____

8. been told that fighting was a part of
   "being a man"?   _____   _____

9. been injured and said, "It doesn't hurt," when
   you really were in pain?   _____   _____

10. hurt another person while fighting?   _____   _____

11. hurt an animal physically?   _____   _____

12. hurt a child physically?   _____   _____

12. killed an animal?   _____   _____

13. killed another person?   _____   _____

13. been in the military?   _____   _____

14. been a member of law enforcement?   _____   _____

15. been arrested for a "violent" crime?   _____   _____

16. been wounded by a weapon?   _____   _____

17. been in a gang?   _____   _____

18. fought because you were afraid your friends
    would think you were weak if you didn't?   _____   _____

19. seen violence resolve a dispute?   _____   _____

EXERCISE 2.3: COMMON BONDS
OF THE EXPERIENCE OF VIOLENCE

Process Questions

1. What feelings came up for you during the group discussion and how have you handled those during your life?_____

_____

_____

_____

_____

2. Did you think there would be so many experiences in common? Why or why not?_____

_____

_____

_____

_____

3. Describe one personal experience of violence that was shared by someone else in the group. How did it feel to know that others had shared this experience?_____

_____

_____

_____

_____

4. Describe one personal experience of violence that was not shared by someone else in the group. How did it feel to be the only one who has had this experience? _____

_____

_____

_____

_____

5. Do you think people have had similar experiences and have chosen not to be violent with their partners? Why or why not?

_____

_____

_____

_____

6. How can you help to create a different environment in your own family?_____

_____

_____

_____

_____

7. How can you define yourself (as a male) without using violence as part of the definition?_____

_____

_____

_____

_____

8. Having completed this exercise, how much does past experience influence your current behaviors, feelings, and attitudes? Who is in control of how much the past influences you?_____

_____

_____

_____

_____

Exercise 2.4
Nonviolence

Article Homework Assignment

Purpose: Often, people who choose controlling and abusive behaviors blame others for their behavior. It is also common to hear phrases such as, "My abuse was a one time thing," or, "I was targeted by the police. This isn't a serious problem." If you pay attention, almost every day there is something in the newspaper about an incident of domestic violence. Sadly, to make the paper, the incident usually must end in the death of the spouse/victim, the children, and at times, the batterer. Participating in this exercise can help broaden the experience of domestic violence and can help individuals see not only the scope of the problem, but also the deadly consequences and possible solutions.

Materials: Article Worksheet to be completed and attached to an article that you have found in a magazine or newspaper.

Procedure: Find a recent newspaper, magazine, or Internet article dealing with an incident of domestic violence. Answer the questions on the worksheet and bring your information to the group. In the group, you may want to read the article or give a summary and read your responses to the article. Often it is easier to discuss other people's problems while planting seeds for future group discussions and activities regarding nonviolence. This exercise also assists in building empathy for victims, and makes us realize that domestic violence occurs more often than we think. Examining and realizing how and to what extent domestic violence effects others can be a doorway to looking at your own abusive and controlling behaviors. As we mentioned earlier, it is often less threatening to look at someone else's experiences before examining your own.

EXERCISE 2.4: ARTICLE WORKSHEET

Name:_____ Topic:_____

1. Why did you pick this article?_____

   _____

   _____

2. What happened?_____

   _____

   _____

3. Who was involved?_____

   _____

4. Who was a victim?_____

   _____

5. Who was the perpetrator?_____

   _____

6. Who else was affected in this incident besides the victim?_____

   _____

   _____

7. How were they affected?_____

   _____

   _____

8. What could the perpetrator have done differently that would be
   nonviolent and/or nonabusive?_____

   _____

   _____

   _____

   _____

Chapter 3

EXPLORING AND DEFEATING INTIMIDATION

I n working with battering groups, we have been surprised to find how few of the group members consider themselves intimidating to others. In one exercise that is done in group, we would have a few group members role-play intimidating postures and gestures with other group members. Believe it or not, they had a hard time completing the role-play. They said "This is too hard" or "I can't do this. I'm not a scary guy." What surprised us was their lack of recognition about just how intimidating they actually were, not only to women, but also to other men.

Intimidation is much more sinister than the overt violence discussed in Chapter 2, because intimidation can be denied by the person doing the intimidating. For example, one guy in group was over six feet tall and weighed about 270 pounds. The man was intimidating by virtue of his size. He would say, "Look, there's nothing I can do about that." He's right. He can't change his size, but he can recognize that his size could influence how other people perceive and act around him. Once you have that recognition, you can use that insight to consider how others are feeling and change how you approach people based on this knowledge.

Whether it is use of size, scary eye contact, wild hand gestures, or an intrusion of personal space, intimidation is used as an effective means of control in many relationships. The exercises in this chapter are formulated to examine various aspects of intimidation, and provide a few techniques for change. Two stories from actual group members are provided to give a real life perspective on the struggle other people go through to modify their intimidating beliefs and behaviors.

Exercise 3.1
Exploring and Defeating Intimidation

Adam's Story

I grew up where there were only two kinds of people. Either you were Black or you were a redneck. When I was growing up we learned to fight to survive. It was the way of life. I remember my first time to settle an argument with my fists, I was about eight years old. My Dad and my brothers were proud of me, I kicked some older kid's ass. It was the way we lived. I was expected to be tough and fight my way through life. I am now beginning to understand I have to change my whole way of thinking and believing or I am going to lose my wife and family. I have been to about 10 groups now and something happened last week for the first time in my life.

I'm a truck driver. I am totally dependent financially on my truck to support my family. I was parked last Sunday taking a break, eating my lunch in my cab and felt my trailer being hit from behind, not real hard but I knew someone hit me. I opened my door and when my foot hit the pavement, for the first time in my life I knew I wasn't going to be violent with this individual. I walked calmly to the back of the truck, didn't say anything. Because of my size I knew this guy would be scared of me. I looked at the small dent. The other guy was full of apologies. He seemed scared to death because he was a lot smaller than me. I told him, 'don't worry about it. I'll take care of it.' I walked back to my cab, got in and left.

A year ago I would have walked around to the back and beat the guy bloody into the ground and then left. I would not have asked any questions. I felt good about myself for the first time. I controlled myself. I was really proud of what I did. A year ago I would have gone to jail again, paid fines, and had more probation. But not this time—I am learning to do things different.

EXERCISE 3.1: ADAM'S STORY

Processing Questions

1. How do Adam's early life experiences compare to your own?_____

   _____

   _____

   _____

   _____

   _____

   _____

2. What changes has Adam made in his life? What changes does he
   still need to make?_____

   _____

   _____

   _____

   _____

   _____

3. What are some alternatives for handling the situation Adam
   confronted?_____

   _____

   _____

   _____

   _____

   _____

   _____

Exercise 3.2
Exploring and Defeating Intimidation

Supper Time!

Purpose: For many families, the hub of communication centers around the kitchen, and the traditional meeting place is around the dinner table. In fact, the ritual of eating can be either a very happy time, or a time that is filled with confrontation. Whether or not your family gathered around a table is not as important as how you remember your family congregating during the evening hours. Try to picture in your mind the feeling of supper time. Was it a happy time of day? Sad? Frightening? This activity may draw out powerful memories and there may be the need to process painful childhood memories of abuse or neglect. It will also help you see how patterns forged in your childhood are continuing due to choices you make with your present family. This activity is one way begin to understand where you learned many of your own abusive behaviors and attitudes and how these behaviors and attitudes have been changed or modified over time. This exercise was adapted to battering groups from a general exercise by Trotzer (1997).

Materials: Supper Time! Worksheets.

Procedure:

1. Draw the room where your family ate supper when you were 10 years old, from a bird's eye view (looking down on the room from the ceiling). Draw the top of the table, TV trays, how the chairs were arranged.

2. Write in who ate with you. Place them in their usual places.

3. Imagine each person's personality during this time in your life. Answer the following questions on the worksheet.

   • Who did you like? Not like?

   • Who were you afraid of? Who was afraid of you?

   • Was anybody regularly missing from supper time? Why?

   • What was the general feeling about being with the family during this time for each person?

   • If you could think of one sentence that each person could say that would sum up his or her image, what would it be?

4. Now draw the supper time meeting for your present family. What has changed? What hasn't changed?

5. What are some steps you can take to improve supper time for your family?

EXERCISE 3.2: SUPPER TIME! WORKSHEET

10 years old

EXERCISE 3.2: SUPPER TIME! WORKSHEET

Present Family

Exercise 3.3
Exploring and Defeating Intimidation

Roger's Story

Roger shared his story with the group the week after we had done the "Supper Time!" exercise.

> I felt awful after we left group last week. I got sick to my stomach and had a headache.

> It was hard for me to remember when I was 10 years old. I have tried to block out my whole childhood, the horrible memories of how my father treated us. When I drew our table and remembered what it was like to be a child in my home, I was flooded with feelings and memories of those terrible years.

> My Dad was the dictator and for any infraction of the "rules" you were beat and cussed at, all of my childhood. I lived terrified of my Dad. Last week I remembered I swore to myself when I was a kid I would never be like him, but then I realized I am just like him.

> (With tears in his eyes, Roger continued) I now realize what I have to do, I have to want to be different more than anything else. I have a long way to go. I don't want to be like my Dad.

EXERCISE 3.3: ROGER'S STORY

Dad and Me Worksheet

Like Roger, many men are heavily influenced by their fathers. The worksheet below is designed to help you explore the similarities and differences in you and your father. This exercise is not intended to be done only once, but is a worksheet that you can add items to as you learn more about yourself.

Dad is . . .	I am . . .
1.	
2.	
3.	
4.	
5.	
6.	
7.	
8.	
9.	
10.	
11.	
12.	
13.	
14	
15.	
16.	

EXERCISE 3.3: ROGER'S STORY

Processing Questions

1. Using your answers from the "Dad and Me" exercise on the previous page, what characteristics do you share with your father? What characteristics are not the same?_____

_____

_____

_____

_____

2. What aspects of Roger's dad were intimidating? _____

_____

_____

_____

3. List some of your own characteristics and behaviors that you feel intimidate others. Include characteristics of yourself that others (children, your partner, friends) have told you are intimidating.

_____

_____

_____

_____

4. Interview three group members or friends and ask them to list anything about you that they find intimidating or threatening. Write below what they say._____

_____

_____

_____

_____

_____

Exercise 3.4
Exploring and Defeating Intimidation

Time-Out vs. Walking Away

Purpose: Many group members discuss their anger as "losing control" or getting pushed to the "point of no return." Anger management strategies are designed to help the individual realize that his or her anger is a choice and is under each person's own control. In abusive and controlling relationships, the anger is not the problem, it is how one deals with one's anger. People in abusive relationships use anger and violence to control another person. Saying "I was just out of control" is just an excuse to not take responsibility for your feelings and actions. Taking a time-out is a structured way to take responsibility for your anger or other feelings and take steps to remedy the situation. If you have children, you might be aware of what a time-out looks like. This exercise outlines the difference between taking a time-out and just walking away from conflict.

Materials: Time Out vs. Walking Away Differences Chart; Steps of an Effective Time-Out; Time-Out Processing Form; John's Story; Processing John's Story; and the Self Statements List.

Procedure: First, examine the difference between time-outs and walking away from a conflict, and try to apply each strategy to conflict that you have had in the past. Consider the advantages and disadvantages of each approach. Read over the steps for time-out and discuss them with your group and your partner. Make sure you ask any questions you may have about how to use a time-out effectively. A sample case story has been supplied for you to consider. John's story is to be used as practice in understanding and then using the steps. The Time-Out Processing Form and the Self Statements List are to be used when you have an incident at home or work and you feel like you need a time-out.

EXERCISE 3.4: TIME-OUT VS. WALKING AWAY

Differences Chart

This outline is designed to give you a clear idea of the difference between deciding to take a time-out during an argument and just walking away (leaving the room, house, etc.).

TIME-OUT	WALKING AWAY
1. You can identify your feelings.	1. You are uncertain of your feelings.
2. You communicate with your partner about your feelings.	2. Your partner is confused about what's going on with you.
3. Is an agreed upon strategy between you and your partner and was discussed before conflict occurs (proactive).	3. Is often not an agreed upon strategy between you and your partner and happens spontaneously. (Reactive)
4. You take responsibility for your feelings, beliefs and actions during the conflict.	4. You blame your partner for making you angry and/or believe your partner is unreasonable.
5. The intent is conflict resolution.	5. The intent is conflict avoidance.
6. Time away is spent focusing on self and working to solve an issue.	6. Time away is spent blaming partner and behaviors that hurt the relationship (drinking, pouting, slamming doors).
7. You return with ideas for change that are focused on ways you can do things differently.	7. You return either more angry and frustrated than you were before or you want to avoid the issue. "I hope it just blows over if I can lay low."

EXERCISE 3.4: TIME-OUT VS. WALKING AWAY

Steps of an Effective Time-Out

1. **Understand the differences between a time-out and walking away from an argument.** Once you understand the differences, a commitment must be made to following through and believing in the time-out process. Thinking it won't help will lead to you not putting the effort that is required to make it effective.

2. **Discuss the idea of time-out with your partner.** Go over the differences between time-outs and walking away. Time-outs should be discussed as a strategy for *you*. The idea should not be a mandate that you are requiring of everyone in the family. If your partner wants to try time-outs too, great. However the emphasis is on how you want support in ways that you are trying to change your behavior. The second part of this step is to discuss the idea of time-outs *before* not *during* a conflict. By sitting down and discussing ideas at a calm, agreed upon time you both can explore the issue in a cooperative manner.

3. **Once you both understand what a time-out is** and how you are going to use it, you are ready to use time-outs during conflicts. During an argument, **pay attention to your physical and situational cues of anger.** When you feel them escalating say something like, "I am feeling angry. I would like to take a (fill in time amount) time-out."

4. **Go to a place where you can sit quietly, relax, and consider your thoughts and feelings.** For some people, walking around the block or other forms of exercise can be helpful as long as you are able to think about the issues of the conflict. Refrain from exercise that is violent in nature (chopping trees, hammering, hitting pillows, etc.). This behavior can be very intimidating to your partner.

5. **Use the Time-Out Processing Form and the Self Statements List during the time-out.**

6. **Return and ask to discuss the issue when your partner is ready.**

EXERCISE 3.4: TIME-OUT VS. WALKING AWAY

John's Story

Use the story below to process the questions concerning time-outs.

I have been married for four years. I don't know, it just seems like me and Amy fight about the same things over and over again. Take yesterday for instance. I came home and she was real mad because two bills were due. She called me a "no good, lazy bum" and said that I didn't take care of the family. That really got under my skin, so I yelled, "Shut the hell up! You're the one doin' nothin' all day!"

I could feel myself getting real angry, but she didn't care. She just kept on yelling, screaming, and crying. I threw the checkbook at her and called her some names I can't remember. She should have known I was angry and just dropped the issue but she didn't. I said, "Fine. You don't appreciate me? I'll just leave."

I walked out and went over to my friend's house. After a few beers and a few hours, I went home and went to sleep. We haven't talked since and I bet we argue about the same thing next week. It's crazy.

EXERCISE 3.4: TIME-OUT VS. WALKING AWAY

Processing John's Story

1. Did John use a time-out or walking away? Using the Time-Out vs. Walking Away Differences Chart, explain your answer._____

   _____

   _____

   _____

2. Discuss how John could have used a time-out? When? What might have been different?_____

   _____

   _____

   _____

   _____

EXERCISE 3.4: TIME-OUT VS. WALKING AWAY

Time-Out Processing Form

This form can be used every time you take a time-out. Once you get used to the process, you will process the questions in your head automatically, but for now, use the worksheet.

1. What are some of your feelings right now and during the argument?

   _____

   _____

   _____

   _____

2. What are some of your thoughts about the situation? How are these thoughts interfering or helping with solving the issue?

   _____

   _____

   _____

3. Examine the thoughts concerning yourself. What do you see as your role in the problem?_____

   _____

   _____

   _____

   _____

4. What steps can you take to change *your* beliefs or actions relating to this problem? Remember: You can only control yourself. You cannot control another person. _____

   _____

   _____

   _____

   _____

EXERCISE 3.4: TIME-OUT VS. WALKING AWAY

Self Statements List

This is a list of positive self statements that you can read to yourself as you are trying to find a cooperative solution to the issue that you and your partner are confronting. Generate your own list as you think of statements that may help you.

1. I cannot control another person. I can only control myself.

2. I do not have to win this argument. My goal is not to win, but to cooperate.

3. There is value in listening to my partner. We both have important ideas to contribute.

4. I am not responsible for solving all of our problems. The strength of a partnership is in the cooperation of its members. To feel the strength of my partnership, I must be open to my partner's ideas, thoughts, and feelings.

5. I am a responsible human being. My willingness to take a time-out demonstrates a personal attempt to think positively about the conflict.

6. It's okay if I don't know the answer or if I feel insecure about the situation. That's normal.

7. I can handle criticism. I am not perfect.

8. I can remain calm.

9. My anger is a choice. I realize I can choose to be abusive, but I can also choose to be cooperative. My actions, thoughts, and feelings are mine to choose.

10. I realize that if I am angry, then I am either afraid or in pain. I accept both of these feelings and can take a closer look at them when I choose to.

11. Taking a time-out is not a sign of weakness, but of strength, courage, and commitment.

12. Each time I am non-abusive and non-controlling, I recognize the effort I am putting into rebuilding myself and my relationship.

Chapter 4

CREATING A
TRUSTING RELATIONSHIP

Trust seems to be a vital component of any relationship. It is hard for any of us to think about any of our close relationships without trust. Trust for many people means relying on them for the basics in a relationship: safety, shelter, and support. Underlying trust is a willingness to be vulnerable in the presence of your partner. There is a hidden danger, sometimes not so hidden, of trusting someone: The danger that the person you trust will let you down, betray you, hurt you, and abandon you are all possible consequences of trust.

In group, many members focus on the consequences of trust as reasons to either not form trusting relationships or, more commonly, to break the trust first before it can be broken by their partners. The old saying, "Get 'em before they get you!" seems to be playing out in many relationships. Affairs, lies, and abuse are all active ways to dismantle the trust in one's relationship.

Other group members seem overwhelmed by the fear of being betrayed by their partners. Their own insecurities, usually unfounded and based in myth and fear, can lead to trying to cut their partners off from the outside world, jealousy, and stalking. The exercise "Sam's Story" explores the mindset of a person who is afraid of losing his partner and the ways he tries to control the situation. It provides a unique glimpse into what happens when we look to others to provide trust in our relationships. Overall, because trust is often the glue in relationships, it makes sense that people who thrive on power and control would feel constantly threatened by a concept like trust. Group members have remarked that you can make someone follow you, but you cannot make anyone trust you. In fact, control, by its very essence, destroys trust.

Exercise 4.1
Creating a Trusting Relationship

Sam's Story

The following is a story of one of the men in a past group. Read his story and answer the questions on the next page. Discuss the story in group.

I've been in group for about six weeks now and I'm confused. My wife left me two months ago and I think she's fooling around. Like last week, she called me and I just knew someone was there because she really didn't want to talk to me. When I said, "I love you," she just said she would talk to me later. I bet someone was there.

Last night I felt the same thing when I was talking to her, so as soon as I hung up I drove over to her place to see if any strange cars were parked outside. I didn't see anything, but she's pretty sneaky. I suspect she's messing around with this guy from church. One Sunday I watched them during church and every once in awhile he would look at her. Then after church she was talking to him for about fifteen minutes. I stood outside until she came out and asked her what was up. She said she was asking him about insurance, but I think she's lying. I mean, why does she need insurance?

I've been asking my four year-old daughter if she's seen any men around the apartment. Whenever I ask her, she gets all scared and cries. I bet that means her mother is messing around. I told my wife, or I guess my ex-wife now, that she shouldn't be with other men right now. She knows it hurts me and my daughter. She just denies it and says that it's none of my business. Well, I think it is my business. When we were together I had to call her every hour while I was at work, just to make sure she wasn't out messing around. Even though she doesn't live with me now, I still have an obligation to make sure she stays true to me. I just don't know what I should do next.

EXERCISE 4.1: SAM'S STORY

Processing Questions

1. What is Sam trying to accomplish?_____

_____

_____

_____

2. List the actions or attitudes of Sam's that show a lack of trust and/or are controlling._____

_____

_____

_____

3. How does Sam feel as a result of his actions and attitudes?_____

_____

_____

Regarding his ex-wife?_____

_____

_____

Regarding his daughter? _____

_____

_____

4. What can Sam focus on to make life more comfortable for him?

_____

_____

_____

_____

_____

Exercise 4.2
Creating a Trusting Relationship

Wall of Obstacles to Trust

Purpose: Trust can be a big issue in abusive relationships. There may have been affairs by either party, whether in the present relationship or in past ones. If you have felt betrayed you may build a wall around yourself so you cannot be hurt. This wall may also keep you from being non-abusive in your relationship. The purpose of this exercise is for you to identify obstacles to trusting and being able to support your partner. Furthermore, it will illustrate how these obstacles can build a wall between you and your ability to trust. As creators of our own obstacles, we are also responsible for finding nonabusive ways to work through that wall of obstacles. As you uncover your own obstacles to trust, you are encouraged to share your findings with the group. You may discover that others have trust issues that are similar to your own and may have inventive ways for overcoming barriers to experiencing trust and support.

Materials: Wall of Obstacles to Trust Worksheet and Processing Questions.

Procedure: Using the Wall of Obstacles to Trust Worksheet, you will notice that each brick of the wall is separated into two pieces. Work through the exercise by using the steps below.

1. On the right portion of each brick, write down an obstacle to trust. An obstacle to trust can be any action, belief, or feeling that you feel gets in the way of your trusting another person. For example, group members have written the following as examples of their barriers to trust: "When she comes home late, I think she's been cheating on me"; "Jealousy"; "Her mother tells my wife she could have married someone better than me"; and, "I've thought about cheating, so she must think about it too."

2. After you have listed all of your obstacles to trust, use the left portion of the brick to write possible solutions to your obstacle. Examples of past solutions have been: "Discuss this issue in group"; "Realize that I can't control her, I can only control myself"; and, "Realize that I'm jumping to conclusions. My jealousy is my issue, not hers."

3. Try to fill in as many bricks as you can with obstacles and solutions. Bring the worksheet to group and process your obstacles and solutions with other group members. Note any possible solutions for your obstacles that other members offered.

EXERCISE 4.2: WALL OF OBSTACLES TO TRUST
WORKSHEET

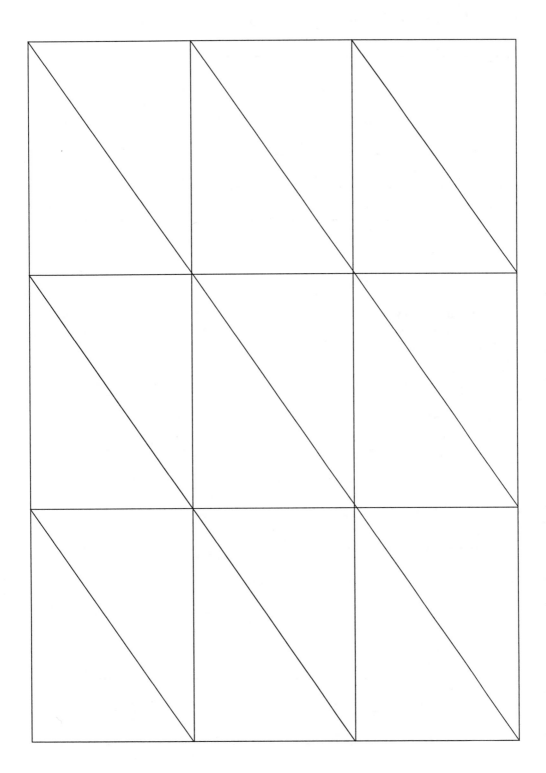

EXERCISE 4.2: WALL OF OBSTACLES TO TRUST

Processing Questions

1. What are the risks of taking down your obstacles?_____

_____

_____

_____

_____

_____

_____

_____

2. Often, when people take down their defenses (obstacles), they feel vulnerable. How can you deal with this vulnerability without being abusive and controlling?_____

_____

_____

_____

_____

_____

_____

_____

_____

_____

_____

_____

_____

Exercise 4.3
Creating a Trusting Relationship

Trust Tube

Purpose: During our experience with batterers' groups, the authors discovered that many of the behaviors used by members when they are emotionally hurt often facilitate a *decrease* in trust within the relationship. The purpose of this exercise is to examine your behaviors when you feel you trust someone, as compared to behaviors and attitudes towards people you don't trust. The exploration of trust will give you the opportunity to decrease self-sabotaging behavior and encourage trust building behavior.

Materials: Trust Tube Worksheet.

Procedure:

1. To complete the Trust Tube worksheet, you will work with the left column labeled, "When I trust I . . . " Under this column, list all of the actions and attitudes you display when you trust someone. Group members have listed items such as, "feel supportive," "tell them my secrets," "am more intimate," "share money," and "let my guard down" as examples of attitudes or behaviors they display when you trust someone. Try to fill up the entire column. If you get stuck, think about how someone would know if you trusted them. How would you act? How would you feel?

2. Next, complete the right hand column labeled, "When I don't trust, I . . . " Under this column, list the attitudes and behaviors you display when you don't trust someone. Examples could be, "am angry," "yell," "ask lots of questions," "get jealous," and "shut others out." Try to fill up the entire column. If you get stuck, think about how someone would know if you did not trust them. How would you act? How would you feel?

EXERCISE 4.3: TRUST TUBE WORKSHEET

When I trust, I . . .   When I don't trust, I . . .

1. _____   _____

2. _____   _____

3. _____   _____

4. _____   _____

5. _____   _____

6. _____   _____

7. _____   _____

8. _____   _____

9. _____   _____

10. _____   _____

11. _____   _____

12. _____   _____

13. _____   _____

14. _____   _____

15. _____   _____

Once you have completed this worksheet, you can go on to the next page and work through the trust tube process using your answers on this worksheet. Continue to notice your trusting and non-trusting behaviors and attitudes in your everyday life and add them to this list.

Examine the drawing of a tube below. This is the "trust tube." The trust tube has a hole in the top, and a rubber stopper on the bottom. The tube is a symbol of your relationship because your relationship is the container which holds trust. The liquid that fills up the tube would represent the amount or level of trust currently in your relationship. Examine your answers on the previous worksheet. Of the two columns, which set of behaviors and attitudes would have the highest chance of *increasing* trust in your relationship?

1. _____

If you answered the left hand column, you are on target. Behaving in noncontrolling ways and feeling good about a relationship almost always adds liquid to the tube (builds trust). Of the two columns, which set of behaviors and attitudes would have the highest chance of decreasing trust in a relationship?

2. _____

If you answered the right hand column, you are on the right track. Even when trust is high, behaviors such as yelling, and attitudes that come from jealousy, will pull the stopper and let the trust drain out of the trust tube.

Figure 4.1. The Trust Tube

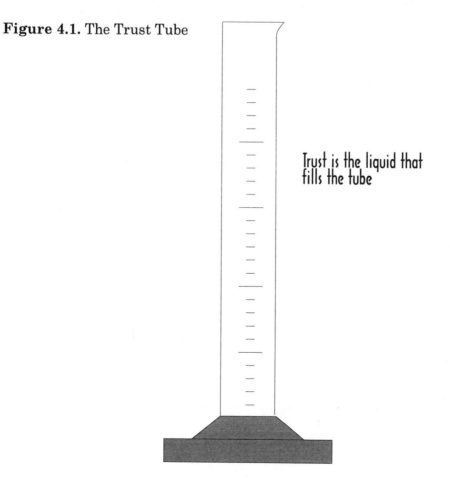

Trust is the liquid that fills the tube

What is ironic is that when most of us need to build trust the most (when we don't trust someone) we do two very ineffective things:

1. We make it the other person's responsibility to build the trust, as when we say, "You have to earn my trust."

2. We think, feel, and behave in ways that actually decrease trust in our relationships, as demonstrated by the behaviors and attitudes listed in the right hand column.

The fact of the matter is, even though you might be hurt by another person, if you choose to stay and work on the relationship, then you are also responsible for filling the tube (building trust). The simple rule to remember from this exercise is, *"If you are not actively creating trust, then you are pulling the stopper of your relationship tube and actively working to decrease trust."* Trust is an important aspect in our relationships, and the better we are at building trust, the better we will be in relating to each other. Waiting for someone else to fill your tube will lead to more resentment.

Over the next few weeks, examine your role in building trust in your relationship. If you are currently in a group, use the group to discuss and process new ways of creating trust in your relationships. Learn from others in your group about different obstacles and pathways to trust. The next exercise in the chapter is designed to help you look at other important elements of trust.

Exercise 4.4
Creating a Trusting Relationship

Exploring Group Trust

Purpose: Throughout this chapter on trust, you have had the opportunity to identify new ways of trusting in your relationships and you have targeted old attitudes and actions that directly contribute to the lack of trust in your life. If you are participating in a group, trust is also an issue that can be immediately explored using the members of the group. This exercise will help you discuss trust as it works within your group.

Materials: The Group Trust Worksheet.

Procedure:

1. Thinking about your group, answer the questions on the Group Trust Worksheet.

2. Bring the Worksheet to group and discuss your answers with fellow group members.

3. After exploring the similarities and differences in the answers on trust, answer the following questions in a group discussion:

   a. What are some ways, as a group, we can work to build trust within the group?

   b. How are the elements of trust in group similar or different from elements of trust we would like to build in other relationships?

   c. What are the co-leader's roles in creating trust in the group?

EXERCISE 4.4: GROUP TRUST WORKSHEET

1. On a scale of 1 to 10 (1 being no trust; 10 being complete trust), how much do you trust the members of the group, not including the leaders? _____

2. What elements have contributed to your level of trust? _____

   _____

   _____

   _____

3. Who do you trust most in the group? _____

   Why? _____

   _____

   _____

4. Who do you trust least in the group? _____

   Why? _____

   _____

   _____

5. How long do you think it takes to build trust in a group like yours?

   _____

6. Using the same scale in question #1, how much do you trust the leaders of the group? _____

7. What has contributed to your level of trust in the leaders? _____

   _____

   _____

   _____

   _____

   _____

CHAPTER 5

GIVING AND RECEIVING RESPECT

Respect, like trust, is something most people would like to experience in their relationships. In processing respect with groups, it seems that the words "I respect you" are seldom actually stated between two people. Instead, group members have said that respect is largely communicated through nonverbal, action-oriented means. For example, one group member related respect as being shown through the following rituals: "There is a hierachy on the job. It's unspoken and it's not written in any of the manuals, but everyone knows it. It seems to be arranged by who's been on the job the longest. They get break first. They get off early if anyone gets off. They've put in their time. They deserve it. I guess we all look up to them for that."

In that example, the workers have arranged themselves by years of service to the company. Service is the criterion of respect. In relationships, the criteria are not so easily discovered. In fact, one popular exercise for this topic is to discuss who you respect and why. In past groups, it was common for group members to list friends and co-workers as people they respected because it was easy to identify why they were worthy of respect: "they worked hard," "they stood up for me," "they were well educated," "they gave me a fair shake." However, rarely did group members list their partners. Why? It would be too easy to say that it was obvious that the members did not respect their partners. After processing the question, we believe it is because the criterion of respect for relationships is too murky. These exercises will provide you with some ways to explore respect in your relationships and give you some ideas on how to achieve a sense of respect between you and your partner—both of whom are worthy of respect.

Exercise 5.1
Giving and Receiving Respect

Emotional Bank Account

Purpose: Emotional abuse can be devastating in a relationship. Often, because the emotional abuse is so accepted by society, men are sometimes unaware that their behavior is harmful to their partner's emotional well-being. This exercise, modified from Covey (1990), is designed to help increase your awareness of what is considered emotional abuse and what the cost can be to your relationship.

Materials: Emotional Bank Account Worksheet.

Procedure:

1. The Emotional Bank Account Worksheet is set up like a financial balance sheet. In the left hand column, you have a place to list your deposits, and in the right hand column is a place to record your withdrawals.

   Deposits are actions that add to the relationship, just like financial deposits add to your money account. Write down all the actions you could perform that would be considered deposits in you relationship. Examples from men in past groups include: a foot rub for their partner, putting the kids to bed, offering to do the dishes, taking out the trash, picking up dinner on the way home, going on a date with partner, etc.

   Withdrawals are any actions that take away from the health of the relationship. Examples may be: yelling, coming home late, getting drunk, forgetting an anniversary, using put downs, calling names, kicking the cat, etc.

2. Complete the worksheet for your relationship and answer the questions on the next page.

EXERCISE 5.1: EMOTIONAL BANK ACCOUNT WORKSHEET

	Deposits	Withdrawals
1.	_____	_____
2.	_____	_____
3.	_____	_____
4.	_____	_____
5.	_____	_____
6.	_____	_____
7.	_____	_____
8.	_____	_____
9.	_____	_____
10.	_____	_____
11.	_____	_____
12.	_____	_____
13.	_____	_____
14.	_____	_____
15.	_____	_____
16.	_____	_____
17.	_____	_____
18.	_____	_____
19.	_____	_____
20.	_____	_____
21.	_____	_____

EXERCISE 5.1: EMOTIONAL BANK ACCOUNT

Processing Questions

In looking over your bank account, you need to consider an important rule about emotional bank accounts that differs from financial bank accounts. The rule, which you may have already experienced in your relationship, is that one withdrawal equals *twenty* deposits. Many men act as if there is a one to one ratio, but reality tells a different story. In reality, you know that calling your partner a "bitch" can not be erased with a bunch of flowers. Outwardly, the forgiveness may seem to be there, but every withdrawal builds inner resentment, fear, humiliation, and anger inside your partner.

1. Based on the ratio above, calculate the emotional balance in your relationship. Record the total below and comment on how you feel about the balance. _____

    _____

    _____

    _____

    _____

    _____

2. List some ways you can improve your emotional balance. Try to be creative. For example, come up with new kinds of deposits instead of just doing more of what you have done in the past._____

    _____

    _____

    _____

    _____

    _____

    _____

    _____

Exercise 5.2
Giving and Receiving Respect

Fear and Respect

Purpose: Why we respect those we respect can be a hard question to answer. For many people, thinking back over our life and those we have respected can help us figure out some basic characteristics of respect. In our groups, men often discuss the relationship between respect and fear. For example, when doing this exercise, one group member reported, "I remember old man Holits. Man, he was mean. He never took anything off of anybody. If you didn't do exactly as he said he would beat the snot out of you. Nobody crossed him. I really respected him." His respect was based on a fear of Mr. Holits. The purpose of this exercise is to examine the traits and behaviors of people you have respected and explore how fear and respect may have intersected in your life. You will also look at who respects you and why.

Materials: History of Respect worksheet.

Procedure: Read each question on the History of Respect worksheet and answer them with as much detail as possible. Some of the questions will ask you to remember people in your past. We know it may be hard for you to remember, but do the best you can. Other questions will ask you to think about how others view you. We realize you cannot read their minds, but try to base your answers on their actions or by how they act around you on a daily basis. Bring your answers to group and discuss them with other group members. Compare patterns of respect of those you respect and those who respect you. Make note of any similar patterns that show a difference between you and your group members.

EXERCISE 5.2: FEAR AND RESPECT

History of Respect Worksheet

1 List some people you respected when you were a child (before age 12). After each name, list why you respected them. Note any that scared you or were intimidating. _____

_____

_____

_____

2. List some people you respected when you were a teen (age 13-18). After each name, list why you respected them. Note any that scared you or were intimidating. _____

_____

_____

_____

3. Out of the people you listed above, how many were bigger than you? How many were verbally intimidating? How many were physically intimidating? How did this impact your respect? _____

_____

_____

_____

_____

4. List some people you respect as an adult? After each name list why you respect them. Note any that are your superior in any way. Does fear play a role in your respect? (For example you may not fear them physically, but you may fear them because they could fire you.) _____

_____

_____

_____

_____

5. Who respected you as a child or teenager? What role did fear play in those who respected you? _____

_____

_____

_____

_____

_____

6. Who respects you now? Why? Of those people, who fears you and why? _____

_____

_____

_____

_____

_____

_____

7. What are some ways you can gain respect without fear? _____

_____

_____

_____

_____

_____

_____

_____

_____

Exercise 5.3
Giving and Receiving Respect

Respect Letter

> **Purpose:** Throughout this chapter, you have had an opportunity to learn about different aspects of respect. Respect is something we, as human beings, want and usually expect from those who are close to us. Like anything else we want, some people choose to gain respect through demands, threats, and violence, while others choose kindness, support, and cooperation. In your quest to become less abusive and controlling, respect must be gained through responsible behaviors, thoughts, and feelings. The following exercise is a tool to help you begin that process.

> **Materials:** The Respect Letter Worksheet can be used as a guideline.

> **Procedure:** Either using your own sheet of paper or the Respect Letter Worksheet, construct a letter to your partner. Go through each question and thoughtfully respond using examples of your own life to fill in the answers. As you answer, be as honest as you can. If you notice yourself deciding not to reveal something, take a moment to think about why you left it out. Are you embarrassed? Are you afraid someone may use it against you? Do you think it will make you look weak? After you have completed the letter, look it over and fill in any pieces that you feel you might have missed. Bring the finished product to your group and read the letter out loud to the whole group or to a small group of your peers. Get feedback from other members on how to improve and modify your letter. Once you are satisfied with your letter, give it to your partner. Your partner is not required to be thankful or give you feedback. The value of the exercise is in the writing and the processing within your group.

EXERCISE 5.3: RESPECT LETTER WORKSHEET

Dear _____ ,

When I was a little boy, what I learned about respect was . . .

I used to think respect meant . . .

Now I know . . .

I am sorry for . . .

In the future I will . . .

I want you to know how much . . .

I want our (my) children to learn from me . . .

I respect you for . . .

I respect myself for . . .

Sincerely,

Exercise 5.4
Giving and Receiving Respect

Examining Group Respect

Purpose: As you know, we encourage you to be active in a group during your attempt to learn how to be less abusive and controlling in your relationships. The group provides an excellent place to process and discuss the various topics that are covered in this book. The group can also be a good place to model and practice the new behaviors, thoughts, and feelings that you are learning. As you learn about respect, you may have noticed that you feel a different level of respect toward the other members in your group. This exercise asks you to think about respect as it is felt and expressed among the people in your group and gives you a format for discussing the difference in a respectful way. This exercise continues to encourage honesty and group bonding.

Materials: Use the Group Respect Worksheet.

Procedure: Keeping your group experience in mind, complete the Group Respect Worksheet. When asked why you do or do not respect someone, make sure you are as specific as possible. Examples group members have given as specific reasons for respect or lack of respect have been, "He is honest about things he's done"; "He listens when I have something to say"; or, "He is too quiet." After you have completed the questions, read over your answers and add anything you might have missed the first time through. Bring your completed form to group and discuss them with your fellow members. While you are listening to other responses, notice how similar or different their answers are from your own. How do you feel about the level of respect in your group?

EXERCISE 5.4: GROUP RESPECT WORKSHEET

1. Who do you respect the most in group and why? What have you done to let this person know you respect him or her?_____

_____

_____

2. Who do you respect the least in group and why? What could you do, think or feel to respect him or her more?_____

_____

_____

_____

3. I believe the other members respect me because . . . _____

_____

_____

_____

4. I believe the other members would respect me more if I . . .

_____

_____

_____

5. I don't belong in this group because: _____

_____

_____

_____

6. I do belong in this group because: _____

_____

_____

_____

_____

Exercise 5.5
Giving and Receiving Respect

Guillermo's Story

I have been married for about eight years. For six of those years I put her through a living hell. We have two little girls. I have been violent, cruel, and destructive throughout the whole marriage. I believed that a wife should automatically respect her husband. As a man, I thought I was entitled to that much. My dad always used to say, "I'm the man of the house. You WILL respect me." He demanded it from mom and us kids and it seemed to work.

When I became a father and husband, I wanted the house to be clean, the kids quiet, and supper on the table when I got home from working all day. I used to get so angry if everything wasn't done to my specifications. I felt like she was slacking on her part of the relationship and that she didn't respect me as a man. I talked about "showing common courtesy" and "my rights as a human being," but what I was really saying was that she should do what I say because I said it.

It seems so silly now. I am ashamed of how I treated my wife. I know my children saw and heard almost everything. You all don't know what I put that woman through. I can't believe she is still with me. I don't know if I can ever make any of this up to her, but I want to try. I believe now that respect is something I have to earn, not something I automatically get because I'm the guy. I have learned to see the value in her contributions to the home. I mean, she has to raise the kids while I'm at work, and keeping the house together is no easy chore. Believe me, I wouldn't want to do it! I also listen a lot more to her opinions on things. I have to admit, our relationship is a lot smoother when I take the time to listen. She appreciates it and I don't get so angry because I don't feel like I have to handle everything myself. It all starts with respect. Not the way my dad meant it, not demanded, but earned.

EXERCISE 5.5: GUILLERMO'S STORY

Processing Questions

1. What did you learn from your mother and father about respect?

_____

_____

_____

_____

_____

_____

2. In your opinion, how did Guillermo's old beliefs and actions impact his relationship with his wife and children?_____

_____

_____

_____

_____

_____

3. List some of Guillermo's new attitudes about respect. Discuss any similarities or differences between Guillermo's approach and your own approach to respect. List your steps in your plan to earn respect._____

_____

_____

_____

_____

_____

_____

Chapter 6

ACCOUNTABILITY: TAKING RESPONSIBILITY FOR YOURSELF

Hopefully, by this time in your change process, you have learned a great deal about your controlling attitudes and behaviors and are making an effort to modify them through your group counseling and the exercises in this book. Unfortunately, many people get stuck in the process. Some group members feel as if they are the victims of feminist backlash, insane neighbors, corrupt police, or the wrath of God. These beliefs stall their possibility for change, and continue to have a negative impact on their relationships and the group. If you are one of those people, then this chapter will hopefully be a turning point in your process. If you are already accountable for your actions, then the exercises will reinforce the progress you have made.

Accountability is the most important part of committing yourself to a nonabusive future. It is working past all of the embarrassment about being labeled a "batterer" and having to come to group. It means standing up and accepting your strengths and limitations, and moving forward. It is not about shame—it's about acceptance and growth. The following interchange between two group members explains the different levels of accountability far better than we ever could:

Lonnie: I don't like being a called a batterer. You can call me anything else, but not that.

Reggie: Man, I don't care if you call yourself the President of the United States. You are what you are. You have to accept it. Quit fighting it and move on! Until you do, you're going to be hating everybody and blaming the whole world for your problems.

Accountability has been referred to as the speed bump of change. We encourage you to work though the speed bumps and make your way to the expressway. Like some of the other exercises, revisit this chapter as often as needed.

Exercise 6.1
Accountability

Defining Accountability

Purpose: Being responsible for one's actions is the first step in any change process. Once you admit you need to change something about the way you feel, think, or behave, you can target the areas for growth. Throughout this book, you have been given the opportunity to take a look at various aspects of controlling relationships that you may need to focus on in your current life. The exercises on accountability are designed to examine how you can recognize and be open about parts of yourself that could change and grow. The focus, as always, will be on you and your feelings, actions, and thoughts.

Materials: The Components of Accountability list.

Procedure: Read over the Components of Accountability list and answer the questions that pertain to the list. React as honestly as possible to what is contained on the list. The components lay the groundwork for the rest of the chapter and so it is important that you discuss your feelings and thoughts concerning the items on the list. Discuss your responses with the group.

Before you read the list, answer the following question:

Question: Define, in your own words, "accountability": _____

_____

_____

_____

_____

_____

EXERCISE 6.1: DEFINING ACCOUNTABILITY

Components of Accountability

1. I, alone, am responsible for my thoughts, actions, and feelings.

2. I use abusive and controlling behaviors to control my partner.

3. Because I am responsible for my thoughts, actions, and feelings, my partner is not to blame.

4. Because I am responsible for my thoughts, actions, and feelings, I cannot blame my past, my parents, society, or drugs and alcohol.

5. I blame my partner because I can. Blaming is another form of control.

6. Because my thoughts, actions, and feelings are a choice, I cannot be provoked.

7. I, alone, own my thoughts, actions, and feelings. When I receive consequences, it is my responsibility, not the responsibility of the courts, the police, the district attorney, or my partner.

8. I realize that due to my abusive and controlling thoughts, actions, and feelings, my partner will be afraid and not trust me.

9. I recognize that my abusive and controlling thoughts, actions, and feelings hurt my partner and my children physically and emotionally.

10. Because I am the one solely responsible for my abusive thoughts, actions, and feelings, I must be the one to change.

11. I recognize that it is my choice to be controlling or noncontrolling.

EXERCISE 6.1: DEFINING ACCOUNTABILITY

Process Questions

1. Which components of accountability do you most agree with or are already using in your life?_____

_____

_____

_____

2. Which components of accountability do you disagree with? Why?

_____

_____

_____

_____

3. What will be the hardest part of becoming accountable for your thoughts, actions, and feelings?_____

_____

_____

_____

_____

4. Review your earlier definition of accountability. After reading the components of accountability, how would you change your definition?_____

_____

_____

_____

_____

_____

Exercise 6.2
Accountability

Your Excuses/Your Behavior

Purpose: Now that you have some idea about how accountability is going to be discussed in this book, we will examine some incidents in your life so you can assess how accountable you are in everyday life. Like many exercises in this book, this exercise can be completed for any incident that occurs in your life. The exercise was designed so you can efficiently be able to discriminate between things that you can change and things that you cannot change. The idea being that the more you focus on things you can change, the more accountable you can become.

Materials: The Your Excuses/Your Behavior Worksheet.

Procedure: Think of the incident which led to your arrest or understanding that you needed to change. There are two parts to every story. On the left hand side of the worksheet, you will see a column marked "Your Excuses." In this column, list every excuse or reason you can think of to explain your behavior. Examples from past groups include: "She was drunk," "I was high," "My neighbors are nosey and called the police," and, "The police had it in for me." Be thorough in your listing of explanations. On the right hand part of the worksheet, you will see a second column marked "Your Behavior." Under this column, list the behavior or behaviors for which you received consequences. Examples from past groups include: "I pushed her down," "I kicked her in the stomach," and "I slapped her face." If you are advanced in accountability, you can also list any thoughts or feelings you are accountable for in this incident. After you have completed the worksheet, answer the process questions and discuss them in group.

EXERCISE 6.2: YOUR EXCUSES/YOUR BEHAVIOR WORKSHEET

Your Excuses   Your Behavior

_____   _____

_____   _____

_____   _____

_____   _____

_____   _____

_____   _____

_____   _____

_____   _____

_____   _____

_____   _____

_____   _____

_____   _____

_____   _____

_____   _____

_____   _____

_____   _____

_____   _____

_____   _____

EXERCISE 6.2: YOUR EXCUSES/YOUR BEHAVIOR

Process Questions

1. What or who is the focus of the "Your Excuses" column?_____

   _____

   _____

2. What or who is the focus of the "Your Behavior" column? _____

   _____

   _____

3. What is the relationship between the "Your Excuses" and the "Your Behavior" columns?_____

   _____

   _____

   _____

   _____

4. Which of the two columns would be most productive to work with in group? Why? _____

   _____

   _____

   _____

   _____

5. If you did the same exercise for a positive moment in your life, say, a job promotion, how would the list be different? Is it easier to be accountable when good things happen? Why?_____

   _____

   _____

   _____

   _____

   _____

EXERCISE 6.2: MOVING FORWARD USING THE YOUR EXCUSES/YOUR BEHAVIOR WORKSHEET

With most group members, as you process the worksheet, some points become apparent. The "Your Excuses" column is usually filled with reasons that point to other people as being the cause for your behavior. For example, saying, "My neighbors are nosey" makes the neighbors responsible for your behavior. In effect, you are saying that if your neighbors were not so nosey, you would not have gotten caught and received consequences. You are targeting the problem as your neighbors and not yourself. Another popular example is, "She pushed my buttons." Once again, the statement makes another person responsible for your behavior and places her as the problem.

How you define the problem is important because it determines how you go about fixing the issue. For example, if you have a boat that is leaking, what you determine to be the cause of the leak will determine how you fix the leak. The same principle applies to personal problems. If you determine that your behavior is caused by your neighbors or your partner, you will look for solutions that will change them or you will ignore the problem because "it's their responsibility." This assumption, and the "Your Excuses" column, violates the components of accountability.

There are many reasons why it is important to focus solely on the "Your Behavior" column. First, to make strides toward accountability, you need to adhere to the components of accountability. Focusing on others, by definition, takes the responsibility away from you and destroys accountability. Secondly, and most importantly, you can only change what is in the "Your Behavior" column. You cannot change your neighbors. You cannot change your partner. You can only control *you*. Excuses for behavior that focus on others may be valuable in the courtroom, but they get in the way of change and growth in counseling. Your group facilitator and fellow group members know you will be more successful focusing on yourself.

Exercise 6.3
Accountability

Intrinsic vs. Extrinsic Accountability

Purpose: The last two exercises were designed to give you an introduction to the concept of accountability and how it is expressed in your life. We have come to notice that accountability comes from two main sources: extrinsic and intrinsic. Extrinsic accountability occurs when you change your behavior because another person or an outside agency gives you consequences for your behavior. In other words, you change because you are avoiding some consequence put on you by an outside force. For example, many group members say, "I'll never hit another person again. It costs too much money." Or "I didn't know the cops took this so seriously. I won't even argue anymore." Extrinsic accountability is most noticeable at the beginning of your change process.

Intrinsic accountability occurs when you change your behavior because you believe it is the right thing to do. Deep inside, you realize that you are responsible for hurting another person and for that reason, you want to change. The Components of Accountability are good examples of what it takes to have intrinsic accountability. A person who is intrinsically accountable will change behavior even in the absence of external consequences. This type of accountability seems to occur later in the change process and takes a lot of work on the part of the individual.

This exercise helps you explore your level of extrinsic and intrinsic accountability.

Materials: Process Questions for Extrinsic and Intrinsic Accountability.

Procedure: Work through the process questions and try to come up with several examples for each question. Bring your answers to group to discuss with other members.

EXERCISE 6.3: INTRINSIC VS. EXTRINSIC ACCOUNTABILITY

Process Questions

1. List examples of consequences you have received for your controlling and abusive behavior._____

   _____

   _____

   _____

   _____

2. Discuss the role the consequences play in your desire to change. How painful are they? Are they no big deal? Why?_____

   _____

   _____

   _____

   _____

3. What other consequences could be placed on you that might motivate you to change? How are these consequences different from the ones you are currently receiving? _____

   _____

   _____

   _____

   _____

4. Discuss how you feel about your controlling and abusive behaviors. In this discussion, explore who and what will have to change for the abuse and control to stop._____

   _____

   _____

   _____

   _____

5. Looking over question #4, if you are the one who needs to change, why? If you targeted someone or something else as needing to change, what can you do about their change process?_____

_____

_____

_____

_____

_____

6. Review all of the questions on this worksheet. Based on your answers, do you feel you are more extrinsically (external consequences based) accountable or intrinsically (internally motivated) accountable? Why?_____

_____

_____

_____

_____

_____

_____

Exercise 6.4
Accountability

Defenses Against Accountability

Purpose: Pence and Paymar (1993) outline three obstacles to accountability: minimization, denial, and blame. If your group uses the Duluth model, then you have had an opportunity to learn about these obstacles. If you're using another program, you might have never heard of Pence and Paymar's obstacles before this exercise. In any situation, a deeper review of the obstacles to accountability are needed to realize the full impact and importance of accountability and how the obstacles act as defenses against accountability. This exercise will examine the purpose of the defenses, the way each defense gets in the way of your achieving accountability, and will provide you with an opportunity to use examples from your own experience to identify the obstacles.

Materials: The Purpose of Defenses, and the individual fact sheets on minimization, denial, and blame, which follow.

Procedure: Read the following section, The Purpose of Defenses. Each obstacle is displayed and illustrates how the obstacle interferes with accountability. The sheet also explains the purpose of the defenses in regard to what the defenses do for you. Answer the questions that go with the different items on the form. Next, read about each defense on its own fact sheet. Try to identify the defenses that you employ most frequently and spend some time reviewing those particular defenses. Give your own examples at the bottom of the fact sheets and consider your strategies for defense. Bring your answers to group and compare your methods of defense with other members in your group. Pay careful attention to all the different ways people choose as ways to defend themselves against the same feelings.

EXERCISE 6.4: DEFENSES AGAINST ACCOUNTABILITY

The Purpose of Defenses

Each of the obstacles—minimization, denial, and blame—act as defenses against accountability, but what are they defending? Think of a castle. If you were building a castle and carved out a moat around the castle, what would you be protecting? Most people would answer "the castle" or "what's inside the castle." Both answers are correct. Defenses, whether a moat or blame, serve to protect a vulnerable object. The moat protects the castle and the people in the castle. Minimization, denial, and blame protect your body from consequences and protect your inner self from feelings of shame, fear, and guilt. For example, using denial and saying, "I never abused her" protects you on many levels. Saying it in court may protect you from jail and fines. Saying it to everyone else may protect you from feeling ashamed and guilty for your actions. The defenses serve the purpose of protection but also shield you from change.

Defenses Block Accountability.   The defenses interfere with accountability in the following ways:

Minimization	Accountability
Is a barrier to accountability which allows some accountability but unconsciously lessens the severity of the action.	

Denial	Accountability
Provides a thick barrier to accountability because the person acts as if the offense never occurred.	

Blame	Accountability
Provides the ultimate protection because responsibility goes off the offender and is placed on the victim. Very destructive!	

EXERCISE 6.4: DEFENSES AGAINST ACCOUNTABILITY

Fact Sheet on Minimization

Description. Minimization is a defense that obscures or clouds accountability more than it avoids total responsibility. It is the person saying that they did do, think, or feel a certain way, but it was not as bad or severe as everyone thinks. The effect on the minimizer is a feeling of *justification*, or that they are actually the *victim*. The impact on the actual victim is they usually feel like they have a made a big deal out of nothing, or they feel guilty for being overly sensitive.

Examples of Minimization.

- Any statement that uses "only" or "just," as in "I only slapped her once" or "I just pushed her on the bed."

- Any statement that gives an example of something worse that could have happened, such as:

  "I punched you in the stomach, but I could have punched you in the face."

  "I took away your checkbook, but I could have locked you in the house."

- Any statement that refers to an accident, such as:

  "I didn't mean for you to land on the edge of the coffee table."

  "It was an accident. I pushed open the door and it hit her."

Your Examples. Give some examples of minimization that you have used in your relationship. What were you protecting by using this defense?

_____

_____

_____

_____

_____

_____

_____

_____

EXERCISE 6.4: DEFENSES AGAINST ACCOUNTABILITY

Fact Sheet on Denial

Description. Denial is a defense that completely distracts the issue of accountability. The person who denies that the abuse or control exists can never change because, in his mind, there is no problem to work on. There is not a starting point for change. In other words, the position of someone using denial would be, "Why be accountable when there is nothing to be accountable for?" The impact of denial on the batterer is *inability to change.* The denial causes *stagnation.* The impact of the batterer's denial on the victim is the feeling of going crazy. In a sense, the batterer is saying to the victim, "It didn't happen. It's all in your mind." This can leave the victim feeling confused, angry, and hopeless.

Examples of Denial. Any statement that ignores the obvious, such as:

- "I do not know why I'm here."

- "I never touched her," when there is a police report, pictures, and eye witness accounts.

- "We never argue anymore."

- "She can do whatever she wants. I don't care."

Your Examples. List your own examples of how you use denial in your relationship. Discuss how this defense protects you:

_____

_____

_____

_____

_____

_____

_____

_____

_____

EXERCISE 6.4: DEFENSES AGAINST ACCOUNTABILITY

Fact Sheet on Blame

Description. Blame is the most destructive of all of the defenses. The people who use blame not only deny that they are the source of the problem, but they also place the responsibility for their offense on someone else, usually the person they have victimized. Accountability is unreachable because, like the people who use denial, the blamers do not see a need to change because, in their own minds, they are not the cause of the problem. The impact on the blamer includes feeling *victimized* and *angry*. The impact on the victim is devastating. The victim feels guilty, angry, revictimized, helpless, and hopeless. The victim feels like he or she must take responsibility for another person's horrible behavior and endure the behavior all at the same time. This is exactly what the blamer wants to happen.

Examples of Blame.

- Any statement that focuses on "you":

  "You made me do it."

  "You know what happens when you smart off to me."

  "You freaked out and called the cops. It's your fault all this is happening."

- Any statement that focuses on other people or substances:

  "It's because of the alcohol. I'm normally real calm."

  "My neighbors are nosy. What I do in my house is my business."

Your Examples. List some examples of blame that you have used. How did blame protect you?

_____

_____

_____

_____

_____

_____

_____

EXERCISE 6.4: DEFENSES AGAINST ACCOUNTABILITY

Questions on the Defenses

1. What defense do you use most often? What is the purpose of your defenses?_____

   _____

   _____

   _____

   _____

2. Based on you experience, what has been the impact of your defenses on your partner? Your children? You?_____

   _____

   _____

   _____

   _____

   _____

3. M. Scott Peck (1993) said this about blamers: They are "the people of the lie because one of their distinguishing characteristics is their ability to lie to themselves, to others, and to insist on being ignorant of their own wrongdoing" (p. 38). How does this compare to your own view of blaming?_____

   _____

   _____

   _____

   _____

   _____

   _____

   _____

Exercise 6.5
Accountability

Accountability Editor

Purpose: Throughout this chapter, you have been exposed to the concept of accountability, how you use it (or don't), and you have had the opportunity to understand some of the self-imposed obstacles to reaching accountability. In this exercise, you will work with your own statements of accountability and edit them for the defenses of minimization, denial, and blame. You will also be given the opportunity to make your statements "more accountable." The editing technique learned here can then be generalized to every incident in your life where you have the opportunity to embrace or avoid being responsible for your own actions.

Materials: Accountability Editor Worksheet, the other worksheets in the chapter for review.

Procedure: On the Accountability Editor Worksheet, list four statements of accountability starting with the phrase, "I am accountable for . . ." Most people think of the most recent abusive incident for their example. After you have written your four statements of accountability, review the defenses to accountability from the last chapter. For each of your statements, edit them for evidence of minimization, denial, and/or blame. By edit, we mean cross out the words that demonstrate the defense and label it either minimization, denial, or blame. Once you have edited every sentence, rewrite each sentence to make it more accountable. The way you make a statement more accountable is to replace the words of minimization, denial, and blame with accountable words that demonstrate responsibility. After you have completed the sentences, bring them to group and have some group members proofread and make comments on your editing work.

> **Original Statement:** I am accountable for onlly slapping her when she hit me first.

> **Edited Statement:** I am accountable for slapping her. (Minimization and blame.)

> **Rewrite:** I am accountable for slapping her.

EXERCISE 6.5: ACCOUNTABILITY EDITOR WORKSHEET

Write your four statements below, beginning with the words, "I am accountable for . . . " Make sure to leave enough room for editing. Your group members can write their critiques of your work under the "Group Review" heading.

1. _____

_____

_____

Rewrite: _____

_____

_____

Group Review: _____

_____

_____

2. _____

_____

_____

Rewrite: _____

_____

_____

Group Review: _____

_____

_____

3. _____

_____

_____

Rewrite: _____

_____

_____

Group Review: _____

_____

_____

4. _____

_____

_____

Rewrite: _____

_____

_____

Group Review: _____

_____

_____

Exercise 6.6
Accountability

Jim's Story

It all started about six months after we got married. We just didn't seem to click anymore. We were always arguing and stuff. You know, fighting and yelling. Well, anyway, she knows that I like to go fishing on Saturdays. I mean, every Saturday that she's known me, I go fishing. This one Saturday she announced that her mother was coming and she needed help watching the kids while she cleaned up. I told her that Saturdays were for fishing and that I already had plans. She went through the roof! She started yelling at me and calling me names. I told her she was being a real bitch. I knew that would really piss her off, and it did! She picked up my fishing gear and threw it into the back of my truck. Well, no one touches my stuff. I pushed her away from the truck and told her to get the hell away from me. She just kept nagging at me so I had to backhand her. I said, "See what happens when you piss me off?" I mean, if she would have just stuck to the game plan and let me go fishing it wouldn't have gone down like that.

She said she was going to call the cops so I tore out the phone. For a minute I thought it was pretty funny. She looked pretty surprised. But then I thought about having to pay for a new phone and I was really mad then. Not only did she cost me a fishing day, but she also made me have to buy a new phone. Anyways, she ran to a neighbor's house and called the cops and I was arrested. She must have had a real wild hair day to go after me like that. All I wanted to do was go fishing and I barely touched her.

Due to her big fit, I had to pay $400 in fines and sign up for counseling. I figure it's going to end up costing me about $1,500 by the time this is all over. She's going to need to get a job to make up the money I'm going to lose. We don't fight at all now. Both of us realize it's not worth the money to get all worked up like we used to. Since she'd decided to leave me alone, I don't see why I need this counseling stuff.

EXERCISE 6.6: JIM'S STORY

Process Questions

1. List examples of extrinsic accountability in Jim's story._____

_____

_____

_____

2. List examples of intrinsic accountability in Jim's story._____

_____

_____

_____

3. List sentences that demonstrate the defense of denial in Jim's story. Edit the sentences to make them more accountable._____

_____

_____

_____

_____

_____

4. List sentences that demonstrate the defense of minimization. Edit the sentences to make them more accountable._____

_____

_____

_____

_____

_____

5. List sentences that demonstrate the defense of blame. Edit the sentences to make them more accountable. _____

_____

_____

_____

_____

_____

_____

6. How could being more accountable help Jim? His wife? His children?

_____

_____

_____

_____

_____

_____

7. How is Jim's level of accountability similar to or different from your own?_____

_____

_____

_____

_____

_____

_____

Chapter 7

MAINTAINING POSITIVE SEXUAL RELATIONSHIPS

Sexual relationships have always been one of the hardest topics to cover in our leading of battering groups. The primary reason has been a consistent resistance on the part of the groups to discuss this topic in a comprehensive and accountable manner. The defenses are on alert for this topic, which typically covers everything from sexual abuse to pornography to rape. Many group members seem to come to the conclusion that if we discuss a topic, then we (the leaders) are assuming the members have the problem we are discussing. In this case, the belief is translated into "If we discuss rape, you must think we're rapists." It is unfortunate that such an important topic area is undermined due to this defensiveness.

The exercises in this chapter are aimed at working around those defenses and targeting areas that all group members can relate to concerning sexual relationships. Each exercise examines a crucial element in forming healthy sexual attitudes and eliminating unhealthy attitudes and behaviors. It is very important that you answer the questions as honestly as possible because there can be no gain in lying to yourself. Using these exercises, we have found that you will be able to gain a deeper understanding of intimate relationships.

Because rape is such a devastating form of exerting power and control, the exercise on rape deals with two stories from actual victims. As you work through the exercises and explore your own feelings and beliefs concerning sexuality, you are encouraged to consider what you can do about sexually abusive thoughts and behaviors. We encourage you not because we think you commit these acts, but because you can be active in showing others that you are not going to tolerate those who do.

Exercise 71.
Maintaining Positive Sexual Relationships

Sexually Respectful Behavior Checklists (Pre and Post)

Purpose: Throughout this chapter, you will be given an opportunity to explore the issue of sexuality and how it impacts your relationship. When discussing sexuality with men, they often comment, "I don't have any problems in this department, why do we have to talk about it?" The authors understand that not everyone who is controlling or abusive is necessarily abusive sexually. However, sexual abuse is another means to controlling another person, and developing and exploring ways you are or are not being sexually respectful can aid you in your attempt to change. In keeping an open mind, you can be free to discover new behaviors and attitudes that will improve the respect in your relationship. This survey will hopefully generate some explicit discussion regarding abusive versus non-abusive sexual behavior and how each can impact a relationship.

Materials: Sexual Respect Pre-Inventory (to be given at the beginning of topic) and Sexual Respect Post-Inventory (to be given at the end of this topic).

Procedure: Before you begin the exercise on sexual development, take a moment to answer the survey labeled "Sexual Respect Pre-Inventory." Answer as honestly as possible. You will not benefit from misleading yourself on the survey. After you have answered the survey, review your answers and pay attention to how many answers were circled "Yes."

Once you have finished all of the exercises for this chapter, complete the Sexual Respect Post-Inventory and answer the questions concerning your responses.

EXERCISE 7.1: SEXUAL RESPECT PRE-INVENTORY

1. Have you explained sexuality to your children?　　Yes　No

2. Do you use proper names for body parts when discussing sexuality with your children?　　Yes　No

3. Have you ever thought NO didn't mean NO?　　Yes　No

4. Do you send your children to talk to your partner about sex?　　Yes　No

5. Have you ever laughed at or told jokes that made fun of rape?　　Yes　No

6. Have you ever hit your partner when she was pregnant?　　Yes　No

7. Have you ever called your partner negative sexual names, like "bitch," "frigid," "cunt," "whore," or "slut?"　　Yes　No

   In front of the kids?　　Yes　No

8. Have you ever forced or pressured her to participate in sex with you against her will?　　Yes　No

9. Have you ever prevented her from using birth control?　　Yes　No

10. Have you ever made fun of your child for being male or female?　　Yes　No

11. Have you ever withheld information if you had been exposed to a sexually transmitted disease or the HIV virus?　　Yes　No

12. Have you ever judged a woman by her appearance?　　Yes　No

13. Have you ever made degrading comments about her appearance?　　Yes　No

14. Have you ever lied about your use of birth control?　　Yes　No

15. Have you ever forced your sexual fantasies?　　Yes　No

16. Have you ever forced your partner to watch pornography?　　Yes　No

17. Have you ever pouted and/or sulked if denied sex?　　Yes　No

18. Have you ever made fun of your child's physical development?　　Yes　No

19. Have you ever "bragged" to your friend(s) about a sexual experience?　　Yes　No

EXERCISE 7.1: SEXUAL RESPECT POST-INVENTORY

Are You:

1. When with friends, "checking" out a woman as she walks by, making comments about her appearance?	Yes	No
2. Laughing at or telling jokes that make fun of rape?	Yes	No
3. Calling your partner negative sexual names, like "frigid," "whore," or "cunt?"	Yes	No
In front of the kids?	Yes	No
4. Forcing or pressuring her to participate in sex with you against her will?	Yes	No
5. Using threatening objects or weapons during sex?	Yes	No
6. Preventing her from using birth control?	Yes	No
7. Withholding information about your sexually transmitted disease?	Yes	No
8. Physically attacking the sexual parts of her body? (breasts or genitalia)	Yes	No
9. Lying about your use of birth control?	Yes	No
10. Forcing your sexual fantasies?	Yes	No
11. Forcing your partner to watch pornography?	Yes	No
12. Pouting if denied sex?	Yes	No
13. Forcing your partner to have sex with others?	Yes	No
14. Hitting your partner while she is pregnant?	Yes	No

Briefly Answer These Questions:

What are some problems you have to overcome to be more sexually respectful? _____

_____

_____

Changes I am making to become more sexually respectful:_____

_____

_____

_____

Exercise 7.2
Positive Sexual Relationships

Sexual Mythology

Purpose: As boys grow into men, each possesses an idea about what intimate relationships are supposed to be about. Within this view, each person has an expectation about how men and women are supposed to be treated in intimate, sexual relationships. In our work, many men—like most men in our society—have received information about sexual relationships from very unreliable sources. Take, for example, Ted's remembrance of his early education about sex: "My dad never talked to me about sex. I learned about it from this guy who was 3 years older than myself. He used to tell all us kids about how easy it was to get a girl to have sex. Now that I think about it, I bet he wasn't having sex. He was just talking to impress us and his friends." As we learn, like Ted, from friends, television, and magazines (the most often reported sources), we develop some interesting ideas about sex and relationships. Zilbergeld (1992) noted eight myths that arise from this early learning. This exercise explores each myth and allows you to compare your own sexual learning to the universal mythology compiled by Zilbergeld.

Materials: Sexual Myths questionnaire.

Procedure: Answer each of the questions about Zilbergeld's eight sexual myths of sexuality. You are free to agree or disagree with how the myths apply to you, but you are encouraged to provide examples (evidence) to support your answers. After you have answered each question in detail, bring your answers to group and discuss them with other group members and compare answers and experiences.

EXERCISE 7.2: SEXUAL MYTHS

Myth #1: Men Shouldn't Discuss Certain Feelings

1. List some feelings that you believe should not be discussed or felt. Why not?_____

_____

_____

_____

_____

2. Many men believe fear, pain, sadness, and disappointment are feelings that should be hidden ("I'm a man. I'm not afraid of anything."). How does this interfere with a healthy sexual relationship?_____

_____

_____

_____

_____

Myth #2: Sex Is a Performance

1. What does this myth refer to?_____

_____

_____

_____

2. Discuss a time that you were concerned with sexual performance. How does a "real man" perform?_____

_____

_____

_____

_____

Myth #3: A Man Must Orchestrate Sex

1. What does "orchestrate sex" mean to you?_____

    _____

    _____

    _____

    _____

2. If a man is in charge of orchestrating sex and a woman does not go
    along with his plan, what does that say about the man? The woman?

    _____

    _____

    _____

    _____

Myth #4: A Man Wants and Is Always Ready to Have Sex

1. How true is this for you in your life?_____

    _____

    _____

    _____

    _____

2. Discuss a time when you did not want to have sex. How did you feel
    about not wanting to have sex? (Were you embarrassed, etc.?) _____

    _____

    _____

    _____

    _____

    _____

Exercise 7.2: Sexual Myths, Continued

Myth #5: All Physical Contact Must Lead to Sex

1. How does this expectation impact casual sexual relationships?_____

   _____

   _____

   _____

   _____

2. Discuss a time when physical contact did not lead to sex. Who made the decision to stop? How did you feel about the decision?_____

   _____

   _____

   _____

   _____

   _____

Myth #6: Sex Equals Intercourse

1. Discuss why you do or do not agree with this myth._____

   _____

   _____

   _____

   _____

2. What does "sex" mean to you?_____

   _____

   _____

   _____

   _____

   _____

Myth #7: Sex Requires an Erection

1. This myth only addresses a man's "requirement." What do you believe a woman requires? _____

    _____

    _____

    _____

2. If you were unable to get an erection, how would you feel about yourself? How do you feel women would think about you? _____

    _____

    _____

    _____

Myth #8: Good Sex Is Excitement Terminated by Orgasm

1. Is this "good sex" requirement for men, women, or both? _____

    _____

    _____

    _____

2. How does this myth affect your sexual relationships? _____

    _____

    _____

    _____

Overall: To what extent are these myths present in your own life? How has your belief in the myths changed over time? _____

_____

_____

_____

_____

Exercise 7.3
Positive Sexual Relationships

Rape and Male Activism

Purpose: Rape is an overwhelming social problem. According to the Bureau of Justice (1996), over 350,000 women are raped or sexually assaulted every year. The FBI (1996) reported that 72 out of every 100,000 women are raped every year and the rate is probably much higher because only approximately 37% of all rapes are reported. Why is rape such a problem? Why are women afraid to report? One reason might be because most of the time women are raped by someone they know: 28% by husbands or boyfriends; 35% by acquaintances; 5% by other relatives (Bureau of Justice, 1994). Although most men are not rapists and do not sexually assault women, rape is a subject that needs to be addressed by men. This exercise explores attitudes about rape and ways you can be active in working against rape in our society.

Materials: Processing Rape questions; Judy's story; Rita's story; What Can You Do? Handout.

Procedure: Answer the Processing Rape questions and be as honest as possible. Like the other worksheets in this book, you are free to disagree with any of the points addressed as long as you support and are willing to discuss your position. Next, read Judy's story and work through the questions concerning your reaction to her story. Then read Rita's story and answer the questions following the text. Bring your answers to group and process them with your group members. Pay attention to moments in the homework or discussion when you feel defensive and might be thinking "Hey, I'm not a rapist and I'm insulted that I have to even think about this stuff." When those thoughts or feelings come up, discuss them with the group.

EXERCISE 7.3: RAPE AND MALE ACTIVISM

Process Questions

1. In your opinion, what is rape? What is sexual assault?_____

   _____

   _____

   _____

   _____

2. In your opinion, what type of people are raped? (How are they dressed? How do they act?) Discuss all the characteristics you can think of and reasons to support your opinion._____

   _____

   _____

   _____

   _____

3. Many male fantasies involve having sex with unknown women, often against their will. How is fantasy different from actual rape?_____

   _____

   _____

   _____

   _____

4. Do you know anyone who has been raped? How has this knowledge or lack of knowledge impacted your view of rape?_____

   _____

   _____

   _____

   _____

EXERCISE 7.3: RAPE AND MALE ACTIVISM

Judy's Story

The following account, like all the stories in this book, is true. This particular story takes place in a hospital emergency room.

> I'm not sure what happened (crying). I had just gotten off work at my job as a cook at a hotel restaurant. I was waiting for the bus around 10:30, just like I do every night. I was a mess! I had food all over me, grease and stuff, no make-up. I had on long olive green pants and a big tan apron. I was just standing there, minding my own business when this station wagon came driving up. The guy inside said, "Hey baby, need a ride?"
>
> I remember thinking that his line was the lamest pick-up line I had ever heard, but I've heard guys say it a million times while joking around. I told him I was waiting for the bus and that he should go on. He left, but he circled the block about three times before he stopped again. He said, "Don't you remember me? I ordered the chicken-fried steak? You must have cooked it."
>
> I said I didn't remember him and I wanted to be left alone. He got out of the car and was saying something to me about giving him a chance. I started to back away but he grabbed me and put a knife to my throat. He put me in his car and drove to the alley around the corner. He cut my clothes off, raped me repeatedly, and then dumped me on the street and drove off.
>
> The whole time I was crying and struggling. He just kept going and saying things like, "I knew you would give me a chance." I am so scared. I know who this guy is. I've seen his face. If he's crazy enough to do this to me, what's stopping him from doing it again? I thought I was safe. I must have waited for that bus a million times. Maybe I didn't fight enough. Maybe there was something else I could have done. I don't feel safe anymore. I don't feel secure. I might as well be dead. Why me?

EXERCISE 7.3: RAPE AND MALE ACTIVISM

Processing Questions About Judy's Story

1. How does Judy's story differ or match your idea about what type of person is raped (question #2 on the last worksheet)? _____

   _____

   _____

   _____

   _____

2. In your opinion, why was Judy raped? _____

   _____

   _____

   _____

   _____

3. Discuss some of Judy's feelings about the rape. Note any feelings that you were surprised she revealed. _____

   _____

   _____

   _____

   _____

4. If you were Judy's husband, what would you do to help her? _____

   _____

   _____

   _____

   _____

   _____

EXERCISE 7.3: RAPE AND MALE ACTIVISM

Rita's Story

Rita told her story in a hospital emergency room:

Someone's got to help me! I was raped by this guy I've been dating. I met him at the health club where I work. I'm an aerobics instructor. Tom was a regular in one of my classes and he would come up and talk to me after class and he seemed like an OK guy. He asked me out and we went out a few times, doing normal things like eating, dancing, and movies.

I don't drink, but Tom did on dates. Not too much, but he does drink. After a few beers, he would talk dirty to me and make comments about my sexy clothes and parts of my body. He whispered the comments to me and they weren't disgusting. Most of the time, I just laughed. I thought they were harmless jokes.

This evening we went out to eat and then went walking in the park. We found a nice spot and we sat down on the grass. We started kissing and he started whispering in my ear again. I backed off and suggested we walk a little more. He said he wanted to stay and then he commented on my breasts! I thought that was a little weird. When I reacted he said he was just kidding and started kissing me again. I told him I wanted to go home.

That's when he lost it. He pinned me down on the ground and started telling me how I teased him in class and on dates with my attitude and the way I dressed. I was wearing a black dress and he ripped it off without much effort. As he raped me he said I'm just getting what I deserve: "You wanted this and so I'm giving it to you."

I screamed, but no one came. After he was done, he told me to get dressed and he took me home. He acted like nothing ever happened. I was in shock. I just sat there crying all the way home. My roommate said I should come to the hospital for a rape exam. I feel so weak. The police asked why I let him take me home. I don't know! I just wanted him to go away. I can't believe this happened. I trusted him and he raped me.

EXERCISE 7.3: RAPE AND MALE ACTIVISM

Processing Questions About Rita's Story

1. How does Rita's story match or differ from your idea about what type of person is raped (question #2 on the last worksheet)?_____

_____

_____

_____

_____

2. In your opinion, why was Rita raped?_____

_____

_____

_____

_____

3. How does your view of Judy and Rita differ? Why?_____

_____

_____

_____

_____

_____

4. How does your view of the stranger rapist and Tom differ? Why?_____

_____

_____

_____

_____

_____

_____

EXERCISE 7.3: RAPE AND MALE ACTIVISM

What Can You Do About Rape and Sexual Assault?

1. *Admit it is a problem.*

   As we have explored these questions and stories, rape impacts a large group of women in our society. These women are our friends, our colleagues, our bosses, our mothers, our wives, and our daughters. Realizing how rape and sexual assault disrupts our lives can be the first step in motivating ourselves to do something about the problem.

2. *Don't be defensive when people discuss rape as a male issue.*

   The vast majority of sexual assault perpetrators are male. Deal with it and move on! Just because most perpetrators of sexual violence are men does not mean that most men are sexually violent. In fact, most men are not sexually violent.

3. *Spend time actively working to squash sexually violent myths and attitudes.*

   The fact that most men are not sexually violent could and should mean that most men are working against the men who are sexually violent. Unfortunately this is not the case. Whether it is because we are spending too much time defending ourselves because we think everyone thinks we are rapists, or because we don't want to be considered "feminists," men do not take an active stance against sexual violence. As men, we need to realize that not only are sexually violent men hurting our loved ones, they are also giving men a bad name. As men, we must be more active than any other group in stopping the men who are perpetrators. The following are some ideas for activism:

   - Volunteer time at a rape crisis center.

   - Volunteer time at prison or treatment center that houses sexual offenders.

   - Confront friends who tell sexually violent jokes. At the very least let them know that you don't find rape a joking matter.

Exercise 7.4
Positive Sexual Relationships

Exploring Intimacy

Purpose: During relations with the opposite sex, men's sexual development is often focused on the idea of "seek and conquer." Another problematic belief is that your partner has the responsibility for providing you with pleasure and intimacy. These attitudes interfere with the opportunity to form healthy and fulfilling sexual relationships with others. In fact, having actual intercourse is only one aspect of having an intimate relationship with your partner. This exercise is designed to help you explore the broad definition of intimacy and begin to focus on how you are responsible for creating an intimate atmosphere in your relationship.

Materials: Answer the questions as provided and use the chart for daily exploration.

Procedure:

1. Read the definitions of the various types of intimacy. Using the worksheet, list examples of ways you are currently being intimate in each particular area.

2. Review the definitions of the types of intimacy and your current rate of intimate behavior. Are there any types of intimacy that you are currently not fulfilling? Do you find yourself more focused in certain areas?

3. Review the definitions of the types of intimacy. Using the worksheet, list examples of ways you can begin to be intimate in each of the areas. Remember, the focus is on how you can behave and feel intimate, not ways your partner must behave or feel.

4. Continue to monitor your expressions of intimacy in your relationship and make note of any changes you feel or observe.

EXERCISE 7.4: EXPLORING INTIMACY

Types of Intimacy:

Spiritual Intimacy

Spiritual intimacy is the mutual sharing of values, beliefs, hopes, and dreams. Spiritual intimacy assumes a common moral bond and understanding.

Intellectual Intimacy

Intellectual intimacy is the connection that forms on a thinking, logical level. It is sharing and validating each partner's pursuit of knowledge, and being interested in the thoughts and ideas of your partner, which includes a willingness to listen to your partner's ideas, even if they oppose your own.

Compatibility Intimacy

Compatibility intimacy is experienced in the mutual sharing of work and play. It can be expressed by enjoying doing things together, but can also be expressed through the acceptance and enjoyment of time apart. Couples that are intimate in this form are comfortable with spending time doing separate activities, but also dedicate time to enjoy each other while doing shared projects.

Emotional Intimacy

Emotional intimacy means partners feel safe to express a full range of emotion within the relationship. Feelings are validated and accepted by the partner. However, in an emotionally intimate partnership, the responsibility for expressing and solving emotional issues lies with the person experiencing the emotion. The act of listening to your partner's feelings is seen as valuable and intimate.

Sexual Intimacy

Sexual intimacy is present when partners feel comfortable with the expression of sexual desires or lack of desire. The physical act of intercourse can be mechanical or intimate. Sexual intimacy implies a mutual agreement between partners to engage in intercourse and involves a willingness to understand your partner's and your own expectations.

EXERCISE 7.4: EXPLORING INTIMACY

Intimacy Worksheet

Types of Intimacy	*Present Examples*	*Future Examples*
Spiritual	_____	_____
	_____	_____
	_____	_____
	_____	_____
Intellectual	_____	_____
	_____	_____
	_____	_____
	_____	_____
Compatibility	_____	_____
	_____	_____
	_____	_____
	_____	_____
Emotional	_____	_____
	_____	_____
	_____	_____
	_____	_____
Sexual	_____	_____
	_____	_____
	_____	_____
	_____	_____

Exercise 7.5
Positive Sexual Relationships

Lonnie's Position on Pornography

This story is one group member's view on the impact of pornography on his life. Read the story and answer the process questions that follow.

I was just listening to you people go on and on about porno stuff and I have to say most of you guys are full of crap. I mean, we know we all do it. I first saw the magazines when I was about twelve or so. I found a box of them out in the garage. I guess they were my dad's. Me and my friends used to sneak out there and look at them. Their dads had "secret stashes" too. We used to trade the magazines and call them "our women." I bet that really pissed our dads off, but what were they going to say, "Honey, junior's been stealing my porno"?

I first masturbated to them when I was about thirteen. I'll admit it, I still do it and most of you guys do too, you're just too chicken to admit it. Fantasizing with a magazine has always been easy. You just look at this gorgeous woman and you can picture her doing anything you want her to. She doesn't talk, she don't complain, she's just there. When you're done, you just put her back in the box. It's sad, but true.

I think that's what the leaders are trying to say. That using porno is not real life. I mean, as a kid I used to wonder when I was going to meet these beautiful women with big breasts and no fat. It's a lot different in real life. Real women have opinions and don't always live up to what is in those magazines. I know you guys think that just because you look at magazines doesn't mean you can't love your wife. I'm not saying you can't, but you can't tell me that when you're looking at Miss October you're not wishing your wife could look like that for even one day. It's like you feel cheated, and it's not fair for your wife to be compared with a fake girl.

In my life I have tried to really cut down. I know my wife is really bothered by it and I don't want my son to be exposed to that. To be honest, having that stuff around never really helped me in any way.

*An excellent book to read on this subject is *The Centerfold Syndrome* by Gary Brooks (1995). It is not a man-bashing book, but is instead a thoughtful book on the subject of men and the use of pornography. Using personal examples and examples of men in his groups, Dr. Brooks explores the issue so that it is understood by all types of readers. Men in our groups have really enjoyed it.

EXERCISE 7.5: LONNIE'S POSITION ON PORNOGRAPHY

Processing Questions

1. What is your opinion about pornography? What are the harms? What are the advantages? _____

   _____

   _____

   _____

2. Lonnie discussed finding his dad's "stash" and socializing with his friends over pornography. Discuss your own first experience with pornography. _____

   _____

   _____

   _____

3. Lonnie mentioned trading magazines and calling them "our women." What attitude toward women was being established by Lonnie? _____

   _____

   _____

   _____

4. Why did Lonnie's dad keep the magazines a secret? Where do you keep your "stash"? Why there? _____

   _____

   _____

   _____

5. Discuss differences between pornography women and real women (your partner, your mom). Some are listed in the story. Discuss those and think of your own. _____

   _____

   _____

   _____

6. Many men defend their use of pornography by saying it doesn't hurt anybody. Who has it affected in Lonnie's story? How does your partner feel about it? _____

_____

_____

_____

_____

7. The men in Lonnie's group felt like it was no big deal to use pornography. What is the purpose of pornography? How do you use it? _____

_____

_____

_____

_____

8. Many men report that they have to increase their level of pornography viewing to stay stimulated. For example, you start out looking at "soft" magazines, progress to hard-core magazines, then to videos, etc. Discuss your type of pornography and to what, if any, extent this progression been true in your life. _____

_____

_____

_____

9. Many men feel defensive when discussing pornography and their use of it. Why? Discuss your feelings during this exercise. _____

_____

_____

_____

_____

_____

Chapter **8**

NEGOTIATING
A PARTNERSHIP

The other chapters in this workbook have focused on issues directly related to specific forms of abuse. Chapter 2, Achieving Nonviolence, dealt with the impact of physical abuse. Chapter 3, Exploring and Defeating Intimidation, focused on verbal abuse and ways you could use your physical being to instill fear. Chapters 4 and 5, Creating a Trusting Relationship and Giving and Receiving Respect, explored emotional abuse and ways to be more caring and less humiliating in your interactions with others. Chapter 6, Accountability, promoted taking responsibility for yourself, and Chapter 7, Maintaining Positive Sexual Relationships, examined sexually abusive behaviors and attitudes.

This chapter is the first of three chapters that focus on practical strategies to becoming a more cooperative and less controlling partner.

In discussing the idea of partnership with groups, many group members say, "Well, I'm not going to be the first to change" or "I'm going to feel like a wimp. I'm not giving in like that." In our opinions, that is the mindset of someone who is in the power position and is afraid they are going to lose something if they change. The key to negotiation and forming a partnership is letting go of the "I have to win" mentality. In a partnership, the focus is on reaching a mutual goal, not proving your point or getting your own way.

The exercises in this chapter have been useful in helping men understand the value of partnership and the differences between negotiation done at work and negotiation at home. We have included a few exercises devoted to money because we noticed that money was a popular device of conflict and control for a majority of men in our groups. Learning new ways of forming an equal relationship with your partner, free from abuse and control, can help you and your partner feel respected and valued within the relationship.

Exercise 8.1
Negotiating a Partnership

Partnership Issues

Purpose: When planning to form a partnership, there are many topics, values, and issues to consider. Most often, couples are entranced by the romantic feelings of falling in love, and fail to communicate their underlying expectations about marriage and the future. The following questionnaire is meant as a pre-marital survey comparing your and your partner's attitudes about certain aspects of married life. If you are currently married, the questionnaire can be used with your partner to identify areas where expectations are different for each member of the partnership.

Materials: The Marriage Expectations Questionnaire.

Procedure:

1. Answer each question on the Marriage Expectations Questionnaire. If you are going to complete this with your partner, each person can write the answers on his or her own separate sheet of paper. Make sure you write who is responsible for fulfilling the need and how important you feel each item is in the marriage.

2. After you have finished the questionnaire, compare answers with your partner. Notice and discuss items where a difference in attitude is marked. Although total agreement is not realistic, because each of you are individuals, a large amount of disagreement can indicate a need for better communication and negotiation of needs within the relationship.

3. If you are attending a group, bring the questionnaire with your answers to group and discuss your answers and the expectations you have about marriage. Discuss how having different expectations about marriage can impact the partnership.

EXERCISE 8.1: PARTNERSHIP ISSUES

The Marriage Expectations Questionnaire

After each question, answer with the word or phrase that is requested. Then indicate how important the task or need is in the relationship by using the following scale:

1 = Very important   2 = Somewhat important
3 = Somewhat not important   4 = Not important

1. Who is responsible for paying the bills?_____

   _____

2. Who is responsible for earning money for the family?_____

   _____

3. Who is responsible for deciding how the money is spent?_____

   _____

4. Who is responsible for housework (cleaning, cooking, etc.)?_____

   _____

   What does a "clean house" mean to you?_____

   _____

5. Do you want to have children?_____

   If Yes, how many?_____

   If Yes, when do you plan to have children?_____

   _____

   If Yes, who is responsible for taking care of the children?_____

   _____

6. Who is responsible for birth control?_____

   _____

   What means of birth control will be used?_____

   _____

7. Do you approve of drinking, smoking, or the use of other drugs?

_____

8. How do you feel about going out separately (you go out with your friends; she with hers)?_____

_____

_____

How often will you go out separately?_____

_____

9. How, where, and with whom will holidays be spent? _____

_____

_____

_____

10. Define "love." _____

_____

_____

_____

11. What role does religion play in your life? What role will it play in your marriage?_____

_____

_____

_____

12. In five years, what will your marriage look and feel like? What is your role? Your partner's? _____

_____

_____

_____

_____

Exercise 8.2
Negotiating a Partnership

What Makes a Good Partnership?

Purpose: As you work through the exercises in this book, you have probably noticed that they all aim to develop individuals who can create caring, nonabusive relationships. As you learn and grow, the goal will be to turn your relationships into less of a dictatorship, where you feel like you have to be the supreme ruler and tyrant, and into more of a partnership. A partnership, like any good machine, requires a number of working parts. For example, it does not matter how good your car's tires are if you have left the pistons out of the engine. Let's face it, the car won't be effective! A partnership works on the same principle as the car example. This exercise outlines some vital elements of any successful partnership.

Materials: The What Makes A Good Partnership? Worksheet.

Procedure: Think about your current or most recent relationship. Answer the questions after each element of a working partnership and list any examples from your own relationships to support your answers. Try to think using your "partnership brain." In other words, try to imagine how your partner would answer the questions, if asked. If your answer and your partner's imagined answer are very different, go ahead and write both answers down. Bring your worksheet to group and process your answers with the other group members. Try to get feedback on how to improve your partnership by hearing about the successes and areas for growth discussed by others. After group, process the exercise with your partner. Because listening is vital to every partnership, listen to what your partner has to say about your answers and any feedback that is provided.

EXERCISE 8.2: WHAT MAKES A GOOD PARTNERSHIP? WORKSHEET

1. **Commitment to Self-Responsibility**

   How responsible are you for your own happiness? Sadness?_____

   _____

   _____

2. **A Mutually Respected Sense of Equality**

   What does equality look like in a partnership? Give an example.

   _____

   _____

   _____

3. **Role Flexibility**

   Are there tasks and duties that you believe you should not have to do?
   Why?_____

   _____

   _____

   _____

4. **Two-Way Flow of Communication**

   Whose ideas are most highly valued in a decision? Give an example.

   _____

   _____

   _____

   What are the consequences of the following common belief, "I don't
   have to ask her. I know she would agree with me."?_____

   _____

   _____

   _____

5. Each Partner Has a Unique Identity

How are you unique? How is your partner unique?_____

_____

_____

_____

What are some ways you have placed limits on your partner's identity?

_____

_____

_____

6. Respect of Privacy

List some ways you respect the need for your partner to spend time alone. _____

_____

_____

Discuss how you use your time by yourself. How would you like to use it differently?_____

_____

_____

_____

7. The Ability to Resolve Conflict

Describe how you and your partner resolved your last disagreement. Share your strategy with the group. Did your resolution indicate a good partnership? Why or why not?_____

_____

_____

_____

_____

_____

Exercise 8.3
Negotiating a Partnership

Money, Money, Money

Purpose: Finances are an important aspect of every partnership. In our experience, men and women list "money concerns" as being a high problem area in relationships. In relationships with domestic violence and controlling behaviors, money can be used as a means to control another person and is often stated by group members as, "I make the money, so I make the decisions." Because money does not mean the same thing to all people, it is useful to explore how each of us uses money in relationships. The following exercise is designed to help you begin to think about the personal value you place on money. If you are in a group, you are encouraged to bring your finished activity to group and share and compare your answers with your fellow group members' responses.

Materials: The Money Issues Questionnaire.

Procedure: Complete the Money Issues Questionnaire by completing the sentences provided. After you have finished all of the sentences, look over your answers and look for themes in your answers. By themes, we mean common threads or ideas that all or most of your answers share. For example, past group members have noticed that a common theme in their exercise has been that they are very careful with money, meaning they are in charge of the finances and "no one else touches it." Others have noticed that they don't really know where the money goes because they don't save any and they don't have any plans to save. You can compare answers and themes with group members or your partner.

EXERCISE 8.3: MONEY, MONEY, MONEY

Money Issues Questionnaire

1. I think money is: _____

   _____

   _____

2. When I have extra money, I like to: _____

   _____

3. My favorite thing to do for free is: _____

   _____

4. My children won't have to pay for: _____

   _____

5. People should be able to get free: _____

   _____

6. The hardest thing to talk about related to money is: _____

   _____

   _____

   _____

7. I'll have enough money when: _____

   _____

   _____

   _____

8. If I had "enough" money, which problems would disappear? _____

   _____

   _____

   _____

Exercise 8.4
Negotiating a Partnership

How I Feel About Money

> **Purpose:** Now that you have had the opportunity to explore some basic attitudes about money, you can more deeply probe into the roots of how you use money in your relationship. If you are in group, or shared the last exercise with your partner, you probably realize that people have many different beliefs and expectations concerning money. We have included two exercises on money in this book because money is a safe, yet hot, topic to focus on for negotiation skills. By safe, we mean that money concerns are usually smoke screens for deeper issues. Winning the lottery will not make domestic violence go away. Many group members have voiced the myth of, "If I could just make more money everything would be fine" or "If she would just stop spending, I wouldn't get so mad." Focusing on the money allows people to avoid the deeper problems of blame, isolation, lack of communication, and the need to control. This exercise helps you explore money and negotiation and gives you questions to discuss with group members and your partner. As you learn to negotiate money concerns and appreciate differing views about money, we hope you will be able to apply your findings to other situations.
>
> **Materials:** How I Feel About Money questionnaire.
>
> **Procedure:** Take a copy of the questionnaire home and spend some time thinking about your answers. Complete the form and bring it back to your next group. As you answer, note how the messages from your parents influence how you feel about money today. Also observe how beliefs from society influence how you feel about money.

HOW I FEEL ABOUT MONEY

1. What was your mother like with money?_____

_____

_____

2. What was your father like with money?_____

_____

_____

3. What memories do you have about discussions or arguments about money?_____

_____

_____

4. What did you and your parents do together for fun? How did money impact your family in terms of fun activities?_____

_____

_____

5. How do you feel about the statement, "Whoever makes the money, rules the castle"?_____

_____

_____

6. Do you feel obligated to support your parents? Brothers or sisters? Others? How do you feel about these obligations?_____

_____

_____

7. What were your expectations about marriage and money? How do these expectations compare to your present reality?_____

_____

_____

_____

8. Do you have money secrets? If so what are they? What are you afraid might happen if the secret is revealed? When is it okay to keep secrets about money? When is it not okay? _____

_____

_____

9. How do you handle finances with your partner? _____

_____

_____

10. What would be the perfect solution to the money pressures you have right now? What are the chances of this solution happening? How realistic is the solution? Who is responsible for making the solution occur?

_____

_____

11. List some ways you use money in your relationship. For example, some people use it as a threat: "If you leave me, you'll be poor." Some use it as a means of control by putting a partner on an allowance. Other people use money as a tool for communication by balancing the checkbook together. List all your uses and be creative. _____

_____

_____

12. List some ways you would like to change your ways of handling and discussing money in your relationship. Remember to focus on beliefs or actions that you can change about yourself. _____

_____

_____

13. What are your plans and goals about saving and spending money? Use this sheet to lay out what a budget looks like to you. Compare your budget to your partner's. Bring your budget to group and compare it to other members' budgets. Note the detail and the different levels of planning. _____

_____

_____

_____

Exercise 8.5
Negotiating a Partnership

Negotiating Time

Purpose: We cannot count the number of times we have heard group members complain, "there isn't enough time in the day" or "I can't get everything done. It really stresses me out!" The issue of time and what to do with it seems to be a universal challenge for human beings. For controlling individuals, time, and the stress involved, can be used as a tool of control and abuse. For example, many group members relate how they think they "have to do everything." This perception leads them to make demands on their partners and not recognize their partner's contributions to the family. This schedule exercise was designed to not only teach time management, but also to give you an opportunity to see how your partner works during the week as well. The added bonus is often, you can both find pockets of time that can be devoted to time spent together.

Materials: Schedule Sheets (one for you and one for your partner. You may want to make copies for other weeks).

Procedure: Fill out the schedule for the week. For each time period, list a specific duty that must be done during that time. Notice how you are spending your time. Major areas may include work, family, alone time, sleep, couple time, etc. Using a different color for each category, lightly color in the spaces occupied by each area. The coloring will help you get an overall impression of where you are spending your time. Ask your partner to do the same. Bring your schedule to group and discuss how you would like your life to change. You may even want to construct a new schedule of what you want your life to be like.

	Mon.	Tues.	Wed.	Thurs.	Fri.	Sat.	Sun.
5:00 - 6:00 A.M.							
6:00 - 7:00							
7:00 - 8:00							
8:00 - 9:00							
9:00 - 10:00							
10:00 - 11:00							
11:00 - 12:00							
12:00 - 1:00							
1:00 - 2:00							
2:00 - 3:00							
3:00 - 4:00							
4:00 - 5:00							
5:00 - 6:00							
6:00 - 7:00							
7:00 - 8:00							
8:00 - 9:00							
10:00 - 11:00							
11:00 - 12:00							
12:00 - 1:00							

	Mon.	Tues.	Wed.	Thurs.	Fri.	Sat.	Sun.
5:00 - 6:00 A.M.							
6:00 - 7:00							
7:00 - 8:00							
8:00 - 9:00							
9:00 - 10:00							
10:00 - 11:00							
11:00 - 12:00							
12:00- 1:00							
1:00- 2:00							
2:00 - 3:00							
3:00 - 4:00							
4:00 - 5:00							
5:00 - 6:00							
6:00 - 7:00							
7:00 - 8:00							
8:00 - 9:00							
10:00 - 11:00							
11:00 - 12:00							
12:00 - 1:00							

Exercise 8.6
Negotiating a Partnership

Working on A Budget

Purpose: Now that you have had a chance to learn about partnership and money and scheduling, you can practice your skills in working with a very complicated issue: a budget. Your knowledge of your views of money will come in handy as you work through a budget with one of your group members. The purpose of this exercise is to give you some hands-on practice in working cooperatively with money. The success or failure you have with this exercise can be processed and worked through so you can approach your partner in a way that is noncontrolling when it comes to the finances.

Materials: Budget Worksheet, Processing the Budget process sheet, a partner.

Procedure: This exercise is to be conducted for one month or at least four weeks. At the beginning of the exercise, you and your partner will get $1,200 each in your bank account. You will get the same amount after two weeks. Using your money you will be responsible for paying all of the bills listed on the budget page. Some amounts are listed for you; for others, such as car repairs, you may have to call around and get an estimate. Each week, you are to bring your budget to group and discuss it with the group. Budget discussion between partners must be done on your own time. After each budget discussion write down on the process sheet how you came to that particular conclusion or solution. At the end of the four weeks, discuss what was easy about the budget and what was difficult. Get feedback from your group members on how to set up a budget in your own household with the cooperation of your partner.

EXERCISE 8.6: WORKING ON A BUDGET

Budget Worksheet

	Item	Cost	Date of Purchase
1.	Food	_____	_____
2.	Clothing	_____	_____
3.	Transportation (gas, bus fare)	_____	_____
4.	Entertainment	_____	_____
5.	Insurance	_____	_____
6.	Heath care	_____	_____
7.	Day care	$80 per day	_____
8.	Radiator breaks in car	_____	_____
9.	Money in savings	_____	_____
10.	Cable	_____	_____
11.	Electric bill	_____	_____
12.	Phone bill	_____	_____
13.	Water bill	_____	_____
14.	House payment	$650 per month	_____
15.	Gas bill	_____	_____

16. Credit card bill (list all cards you have)

    A. _____   _____

    B. _____   _____   _____

    C. _____   _____   _____

17. Other expenses

    A. _____   _____   _____

    B. _____   _____   _____

EXERCISE 8.6: WORKING ON A BUDGET

Processing the Budget

Write down how you and your partner decided to spend your money for each of the items listed on the Budget Worksheet.

1. Food _____

2. Clothing _____

3. Transportation (gas, bus fare) _____

4. Entertainment _____

5. Insurance _____

6. Heath care _____

7. Day care _____

8. Radiator breaks in car _____

9. Money in savings _____

10. Cable _____

11. Electric bill _____

12. Phone bill _____

13. Water bill _____

14. House payment _____

15. Gas bill _____

16. Credit card bills

    A. _____

    B. _____

    C. _____

17. Other expenses

    A. _____

    B. _____

EXERCISE 8.6: WORKING ON A BUDGET

Budget Questions

1. How was the budget exercise done in group similar to working on a budget with your partner? _____

_____

_____

_____

_____

2. How was it different? _____

_____

_____

_____

_____

3. Who made most of the decisions about the money in the budget exercise? How was this accomplished? _____

_____

_____

_____

_____

4. What are some ways you can be more cooperative with your partner when it comes to money? _____

_____

_____

_____

_____

_____

Exercise 8.7
Negotiating a Partnership

Frankie's Story

This story was told by a group member after doing the exercises on Negotiating a Partnership. Read his story and answer the questions at the end.

Well, I want you guys to know that I tried my best with this equality stuff. The finances have always been a big hassle between me and Riki. I make the money, so I handle the money right? Well, after being in here and listening to all the b.s. about sharing, I thought I would give it a try. You see, Riki is always bugging me about knowing how much money is coming in and what's going out. I guess she doesn't trust me or something.

To make a long story short, after last week's session, I went home and said, "You want to run the wagon? Fine baby, here's the reigns."

I handed over the checkbook and all the bills and walked away. A few days later I took the checkbook to see how she was doing and it was all messed up (laughing). I mean, there were bills missing, things recorded in the wrong place. I told her she was doing it all wrong. She got mad and asked me for help. I said, "No way. You wanted to do it. You do it!" That will teach her to bug me, right?!

Well, a few days later I went back to the checkbook and guess what? It was still a mess. I walked into the living room and just started laughing. She got real pissed and blamed me for not helping her. I told her she would have to be a real idiot to not know how to balance a stupid checkbook. She just started crying. I tried to calm her down and said, "You see, this is what happens. I give you the reigns and you wreck the whole damn wagon." I told her I would help her out, so now I'm back to doing the checkbook. So, that's my experience with this equal duties stuff. It don't work for me because my wife don't know how to do nothing!

EXERCISE 8.7: FRANKIE'S STORY

Process Questions

1. Frankie felt like he had honestly tried to negotiate a partnership. What attitudes were blocking an honest attempt? _____

   _____

   _____

   _____

   _____

2. A partnership is based on equality. What are some examples of ways Frankie behaved to take the superior position and make Riki feel inferior? _____

   _____

   _____

   _____

   _____

3. One group member pointed out that Frankie set her up to fail. Explain this idea. _____

   _____

   _____

   _____

   _____

4. What are some ways you have set up your partners to fail? Examples can be actual events, or attitudes and unrealistic expectations you have of your partner. _____

   _____

   _____

   _____

   _____

5. What could Frankie have done differently in this situation, based on what you know about negotiating a partnership? Write a step-by-step plan for Frankie. _____

_____

_____

_____

_____

_____

_____

_____

_____

6. Based on your learning in this chapter, what is your plan for negotiating a partnership? _____

_____

_____

_____

_____

_____

_____

_____

_____

_____

_____

Chapter 9

COOPERATING THROUGH GOOD COMMUNICATION

Communication is the act of sending and receiving information. The art of communicating is the ability to send clear signals and the willingness to hear and receive other people's signals. When two people are succeeding at communicating they understand each other's views and both feel they have been listened to by the other person. How often does this happen in your relationship? Have you ever heard your partner say, "You never listen to me!" or "Why don't you ever care what I have to say?" If you or your partner has ever felt misunderstood, then the problem probably resulted from a breakdown in communication.

Breakdowns in communication occur for a variety of reasons. If you are not *willing* to hear what the person has to say, then you cannot possibly get all the information being sent. If you are not *able* to listen because you are distracted by the television or you are thinking of what your going to say in your defense, then you are not getting all of the information. If you are sending signals using abusive or controlling methods (name calling, blaming, etc.) your listener may be less willing to communicate with *you*. Because everything you do is a form of communication, it is important to recognize your breakdowns in communication and work to replace them with methods that transmit and receive clear signals.

Although we do not believe that poor communication is the sole reason for domestic violence, we do believe good communication is an essential tool for forming caring relationships that are built on mutual understanding and respect. This is one tool that can be used in a variety of situations to take the place of old strategies of abuse and control. Because you can only control yourself, we encourage you to focus on ways you can change your communication style.

Exercise 9.1
Communication

Rules of Communication

Purpose: Any relationship involves communication. Communication exists in many forms: verbal (talking, yelling, whistling), nonverbal (looks, facial expression, hand gestures) and written. In fact, there are so many ways to communicate, it is impossible to *not* communicate. Even silence is communicating a message. In your own relationship, you and your partner have ways of communicating with each other that you have both developed and modified over time. In relationships where one partner is abusive, the communication becomes another tool of control and avoidance of responsibility through blame, minimization, and denial. In this chapter, we will explore communication and learn some tools to overcome the barriers to non-controlling communication. We will start with a list of rules that our own groups have come up with over the years. These rules have been practiced by actual group members in their effort to develop a more cooperative communication style.

Materials: Rules of Communication list.

Procedure: Read over the Rules of Communication. After each rule, write down what you think the rule means and then list some examples of how you, in your own relationship, could follow *and* break the rule. For example, if the rule was "Avoid bringing up the past," you could follow it by sticking to the subject at hand. You could break the rule by bringing in "evidence" from the past to support your current argument (for example, you bring up all the past bills when you are discussing one bill in particular). Remember, these are examples of ways *you* could follow or break the rules. Avoid focusing on how your partner succeeds or fails at adhering to the rules, and focus on yourself.

EXERCISE 9.1: RULES OF COMMUNICATION

Prepared by Group Members for Group Members

1. Keep it simple. _____

   _____

   _____

2. You have the power to clarify if you don't understand. Use it! _____

   _____

   _____

3. Go slow and be specific. Avoid vague language. _____

   _____

   _____

4. Take time to understand how each person defines important terms.

   _____

   _____

5. Avoid bringing up the past. _____

   _____

   _____

6. Talk for yourself, not your partner. _____

   _____

   _____

7. The goal is not to win, but to cooperate on a goal. _____

   _____

   _____

8. The most important step in being a good communicator is being a good listener. _____

   _____

   _____

Exercise 9.2
Communication

Reflective Listening

Purpose: Being a good listener is a necessary component in the greater goal of being a good communicator. Tannen (1990) noted that men tend to focus on problem solving when an issue is discussed. This solution-oriented approach has its costs and its benefits. Whereas finding a solution to someone's problem may be nice in some situations, a broken car for example, there are times when the person is not looking for a solution, but instead needs to be listened to and validated. We have found that many group members do not recognize the value of listening. For example, Stuart stated, "When my wife brings up a problem, I tell her how I would handle it. Sometimes she says, 'You're not listening to me!' I don't know what she wants!" The purpose of this exercise is to give members a way to practice the art of listening in a very specific way: reflection of feeling and reflection of content. These two methods will provide the skills needed to start to explore the value of listening and validating your partner's thoughts and feelings instead of solving them.

Materials: Reflective Listening worksheets.

Procedure: Work through the Reflective Listening exercises as much as you can on your own. Bring your answers to group and discuss and practice the techniques with other group members. Yes, it will feel silly and awkward at first, but treat the listening skills as if they were vital skills or information that you needed to succeed at your job. In this case, the job is your partnership and the listening skills are an important piece because they demonstrate a non-controlling form of interaction with your partner.

EXERCISE 9.2: REFLECTIVE LISTENING

Reflection of Feeling

A reflection of feeling is just what it sounds like, a mirroring of your partner's emotion. The goal with a reflection of feeling is to tap into the emotional content of your partner's message and to validate the feeling by restating it. A reflection of feeling helps the person feel understood and listened to, while helping the listener not feel responsible for the other person's feelings. The examples below demonstrate a poor reflection of feeling and a good reflection of feeling.

Example #1:

Lucy: I'm so angry at my boss. She's always on my case!

Mark: Why don't you just quit if you hate your job so much?

In this example, Lucy is frustrated about the way she is being treated at work. Instead of validating Lucy's feelings, Mark tries to offer a solution. Lucy will feel unheard and patronized by Mark. Mark will feel ignored and confused when Lucy does not follow his advice. The next example shows Mark reflecting Lucy's feelings.

Example #2:

Lucy: I'm so angry at my boss. She's always on my case!

Mark: You are frustrated at the way you are being treated at work.

Here, Mark attends and reflects Lucy's feelings. Lucy has a high chance of feeling understood and validated by Mark's response. Notice how, in giving a reflection of feeling, Mark does not have to feel the burden of coming up with a solution to Lucy's problem. This aspect is important because with the reflection of feeling, everybody gets what they want and are communicating at an equal level.

Try the examples of reflection of feelings on the following page for practice with this important listening skill. As you go through the examples, remember that it is not your job to fix the problem. Note the times when you would like to offer a solution to the problem or even blame the problem on the other person. Instead of practicing your old strategies, practice the new skills of reflection.

EXERCISE 9.2: REFLECTIVE LISTENING

Practicing Reflection of Feeling

Respond to the following examples and supply the reflection of feeling:

1. **Susan:**   When you yell at me I just freeze up. I never know what's going to happen next.

   Response: You feel . . . _____

   _____

   _____

   _____

2. **Natasha:**   I want to know what's going on with the money. You leave me out of the process every month and I'm getting sick of it!

   Response: You feel . . . _____

   _____

   _____

   _____

3. **Lydia:**   The kids have been on my nerves all day! If it's not one thing it's another. It's almost like they like to torment me and push my buttons.

   Response: You feel . . . _____

   _____

   _____

   _____

4. **Carol:** It's just that being married didn't turn out like I hoped it would. We are always fighting and in a bad mood. This is no bed of roses.

Response: You feel . . ._____

_____

_____

_____

_____

5. **Angie:** I can't believe my favorite vase is broken (crying). I know it was an accident, but that vase meant so much to me.

Response: You feel . . ._____

_____

_____

_____

_____

EXERCISE 9.2: REFLECTIVE LISTENING

Reflection of Content

Much like the reflection of feeling, the reflection of content also acts like a mirror for your partner's messages. Whereas the reflection of feeling mirrors emotion, a reflection of content mirrors the meaning or theme in your partner's statement. A reflection of content acts as a summary statement that lets your partner know that you are following the current line of reasoning. It allows your partner to continue to express the issue at hand and gives each party the opportunity to clarify any misunderstandings that you might have as the communication progresses. Consider, once again, Mark and Lucy discussing an issue.

Example #1:

Lucy: I don't know Mark. I have tried several things and nothing seems to work. I just keep running into the same thing over and over again. I feel like I have exhausted my resources and I'm not sure what I'm going to do next. I just don't want everything to blow up in my face like it has so many times before. I know there is no way to guarantee what will happen, but I'm tired of thinking things are going one way and they go another. I feel like a failure.

Mark: Don't feel like that Lucy. You're not a failure. I'm sure if you just wait for awhile, everything will turn out fine.

In this example, Mark has a kind response, but it also could be received negatively. Lucy may feel like Mark has not listened to her real concerns and is minimizing the problem. Mark also makes the mistake of telling Lucy to not feel a certain way. This may be perceived as being bossy. Although Mark may have good intentions, his communication may lead to problems. Even though Mark is not in control of how Lucy will respond, he can modify his communication so that the probability of Lucy feeling heard will increase. The next example demonstrates the change that may get Mark and Lucy the communication they desire.

Example #2:

Lucy: I don't know Mark. I have tried several things and nothing seems to work. I just keep running into the same thing over and over again. I feel like I have exhausted my resources and I'm not sure what I'm going to do next. I just don't want everything to blow up in my face like it has so many times before. I know there is no way to guarantee what will happen, but I'm tired of thinking things are going one way and they go another. I feel like a failure.

Mark: You are trying everything you can think of, but nothing is turning out like you expected.

In this example, Mark highlights the content or theme of Lucy's message. With this response, Mark has a greater chance of fulfilling his communication's intent: connecting with Lucy. Mark does a nice job of sifting through all of the words Lucy is saying and then coming up with a nice summary sentence. The reflection keeps Mark involved in the dialogue and lets Lucy know that she is being understood. Reflecting content takes a lot of energy, but that is what being a good listener is all about: focusing on your partner and tuning in to the message being sent.

Try the examples of reflections of content on the next page for practice with this important listening skill. As you go through the examples, remember that it is not your job to fix the problem. Note the times when you would like to offer a solution to the problem or even blame the problem on the other person. Instead of practicing your old strategies, practice the new skills of reflection.

EXERCISE 9.2: REFLECTIVE LISTENING

Practicing Reflection of Content

1. **Jill:** You never listen to me. It's like everything I say is just one big joke to you. Sometimes I get the feeling that you just tune me out. Like I'm some unwanted station on your radio dial.

   Response: _____

   _____

   _____

2. **Gloria:** I don't see why you can't spend more time with the kids. You are their father and are very important in their lives. Just because we are divorced doesn't mean you can just walk out on them.

   Response: _____

   _____

   _____

3. **Yolanda:** I wish you would stop drinking. I know you don't think it's a problem, but you are angry when you drink. You are abusive when you drink, and I'm scared of you when you drink.

   Response: _____

   _____

   _____

4. **Rosie:** I am an adult. I don't see why I can't get a job if I want to. We need the money and I'm sick of staying around the house all day doing nothing. I want to get out and meet other people. You get to do it and I should be able to have a life outside the house too.

   Response: _____

   _____

   _____

Exercise 9.3
Communication

Assertiveness

Purpose: When interacting and communicating with others, we have a choice to communicate passively, assertively, or aggressively. Each mode of interaction has its own verbal and nonverbal behaviors, goals, feelings, impact on others, and outcomes. In working with battering intervention groups, we have found that being able to distinguish each person's mode of communication is very helpful in being able to be a good communicator. The worksheets and questions used as part of this exercise will give you the information needed to decide whether you are communicating passively, assertively, or aggressively, and give you concrete examples of how to shift your mode of communication when needed.

Materials: Passive/Assertive/Aggressive Behaviors Comparison sheet; Case Examples with questions.

Procedure: Examine the Passive/Assertive/Aggressive Comparison sheet. Notice the differences among the three types of communication styles. As you read over the material, think about your own way of relating to others and which style described best matches your own style of communication. Once you feel you have a good basic understanding of passive, assertive, and aggressive behavior, read over the case examples and answer the questions that follow each case.

Bring your Comparison sheet and your case answers to group and discuss them with your group members. Explore how you can change your own style of communication and the obstacles that might make that change difficult.

EXERCISE 9.3: ASSERTIVENESS

Passive/Assertive/Aggressive Behaviors Comparison

VERBAL BEHAVIORS

Passive	Assertive	Aggressive
Allow others to make decisions for you.	Speak for yourself.	Choose and speak for others.
Avoid saying what you think and feel.	Able to say what you think and feel while appreciating the view of others.	You say what you think and demand that others think and feel the same.
Use words to put yourself down or apologize for your views.	Use "I" statements; direct; no games.	Use "you" statements; blame; threats.

NONVERBAL BEHAVIORS

Passive	Assertive	Aggressive
Poor eye contact.	Good eye contact without staring.	Stare, leering, give them the "look."
Weak, whining voice tone.	Relaxed, calm, sincere voice.	Loud, demanding, yelling.
Shifting feet, poor posture.	Squarely facing the other person with confident posture.	Finger pointing, hands clenched, invading their personal space. Could also be "icy cold."

WHAT YOU WANT TO HAPPEN

Passive	Assertive	Aggressive
To give in so the other person will go away.	To have your views respected.	To change the other person's thoughts and feelings.
To have the other person like you.	To respect the thoughts and feelings of others.	To control or inspire fear in order to get your way.

Your Feelings

Passive	Assertive	Aggressive
Controlled, ignored, resentful, intimidated, self-pity, stretched too thin.	Confident, understood, relief that you could voice your opinion.	Controlling, superior, justified, but afraid and anxious that the other person will assert their opinion.

Your Partner's Feelings When You Are:

Passive	Assertive	Aggressive
Loses respect for you because you can't think for yourself.	Respects your views because you state your views directly and respectfully.	Feels hurt and humiliated. Fears you. Feels frustrated and will avoid you. Building anger and resentment.

High-Probability Outcomes

Passive	Assertive	Aggressive
You never directly get what you want.	You get what you want or can negotiate some thing that you need.	You get what you want but you have to hurt someone (verbally, emotionally, physically) to get it.
The only way to get what you want is through manipulation.	Others around you like to interact with you.	Others may take revenge.
You give up, avoid others, and are often under-achieving.	Through your success, you continue to improve your communication.	You increase your level of aggressiveness to get the same results
You are constantly taken advantage of.		You "let off steam" at inappropriate targets.

EXERCISE 9.3: ASSERTIVENESS

Case Stories and Questions

Teresa has a problem with her husband Leo. Teresa believes Leo should be home to eat dinner at 6:00 P.M. everyday. Leo says he will be home, but lately he has been going to play basketball with his friends after work and he comes home around 7:30 without letting Teresa know he will be late.

1. How do you think Teresa is feeling in this situation? _____

   _____

   _____

   _____

   _____

   _____

2. Discuss what Teresa's communication might look like in the passive mode. _____

   _____

   _____

   _____

   _____

   _____

3. Discuss what Teresa's communication might look like in the assertive mode. _____

   _____

   _____

   _____

   _____

   _____

4. Discuss what Teresa's communication might look like in the aggressive mode. _____

_____

_____

_____

_____

_____

5. How would you handle this situation? Why? What is the probable outcome? _____

_____

_____

_____

_____

_____

_____

_____

_____

_____

_____

_____

_____

Marcos has a concern with his wife, Maria. She has been working nights and he works days, so they rarely have time to spend with each other. Marcos is very bothered by this situation, but is unsure of how to talk about it with Maria.

1. How might Marcos be feeling in this situation? _____

   _____

   _____

   _____

   _____

2. Discuss what might happen if Marcos adopts the passive approach with this concern. _____

   _____

   _____

   _____

   _____

   _____

   _____

3. Discuss what might happen if Marcos adopts the assertive approach with this concern. _____

   _____

   _____

   _____

   _____

   _____

   _____

4. Discuss what might happen if Marcos adopts the aggressive approach with this concern. _____

_____

_____

_____

_____

_____

_____

5. How would you handle this situation? Why? _____

_____

_____

_____

_____

_____

_____

_____

_____

_____

_____

_____

Exercise 9.4
Communication

Editing Rick's Dialogue

Purpose: Every time you communicate with your partner you have the choice to be controlling or non-controlling. You also have the choice to be as abusive or cooperative as you want to be. We usually do not tape our conversations with our partner and then review the tape for errors in our communication. People usually just talk and if an argument occurs, most of us walk away without knowing what went wrong or what we could have done to resolve the misunderstanding. As you learned in the Accountability chapter, many people often use minimization, denial, and blame to avoid taking responsibility for abusive and controlling behaviors. This exercise guides you through a dialogue and allows you to correct errors in communication.

Materials: "I Want to Go Out!" dialogue sheet and questions.

Procedure: Read the dialogue between Rick and Lisa. After you have read the whole conversation, draw a line through the parts of Rick's statements that you think are ineffective. Write in what you think Rick could have said to be less controlling, abusive, or negative. At the bottom of the dialogue sheet, there are numbers that correspond to the number of each statement made by Rick. For each statement that you corrected, write what was problematic about Rick's statement and how your corrections make the comment less abusive, controlling, or negative. Discuss your corrections with your group.

EXERCISE 9.4: EDITING RICK'S DIALOGUE

"I Want to Go Out!"

1. **Rick:** Hey, I was thinking we could go out tonight. You know, maybe out to eat and then a little dancing?

   Lisa: I don't know Rick. I'm pretty tired. The kids have been a real mess today and I still need to go grocery shopping. How about we go this weekend?

2. **Rick:** Damn it Lisa! You're always too tired! I just don't get it. What's your problem?!

   Lisa: I don't have a problem Rick. I'm just tired that's all. I told you I had a rough day with the kids and I don't feel like going out!

3. **Rick:** I'm the one who's been working all day. Look, if it makes you feel better, I'll pay for the dinner. Is that what's bugging you? The money thing? It's always about money with you Lisa.

   Lisa: It's not about money! Anyway, I don't appreciate you thinking that I don't do any work around here. Just forget it Rick.

4. **Rick:** Fine, if you don't want to go out with me, then I'll go by myself. I'll probably have more fun without you. I thought that when you're married, you are supposed to do things with your husband. I guess I was wrong.

EXERCISE 9.4: EDITING RICK'S DIALOGUE

Use the space below to discuss the reasons you changed Rick's comments. Discuss how you changed them and why. Each number corresponds to the number next to Rick's statements on the previous page.

1. _____

_____

_____

_____

2. _____

_____

_____

_____

3. _____

_____

_____

_____

4. _____

_____

_____

_____

Exercise 9.5
Communication

Bill's Story

I have to say I didn't want to come to these groups. I thought it would just be a lot of man bashing. But about the fifth or sixth group I started to relax and listen to what was being said. But at first I hated coming here. I hated probation for sending me and I was pissed at my wife for calling the police when I only pushed her down one time.

Now I know it wasn't only pushing her down, it was the whole way I treated her. I thought I was king of my castle and no one was going to push my buttons. I keep hearing what the leaders say over and over again, "You can't control others. You can only control yourself." It may sound stupid to you new guys, but it's true. I kept trying to make her do things my way because I believed it was not only the right way, but the only way.

One other thing—now I look forward to coming to group. This is the only time in my life I have talked with other men honestly about my life. I guess most guys think they should be able to handle it themselves. Really, I didn't know how to talk about what was bothering me, I didn't have any practice at it.

When we tell our stories in here and learn new tools for life, it has made a big difference in how I act at home. Now I listen to my wife's stories and try to tell her how I really feel about stuff that comes up. I have learned I don't have to solve everything, I can just listen and support whatever is going on in her life. I have to admit, I never thought that just listening was valuable, but it is. It isn't always easy, but I notice when I start to get angry, and tell myself to calm down. Before, I would react immediately. Now I slow down, listen, then figure out what I need to do. I know I have a choice and that feels pretty good.

EXERCISE 9.5: BILL'S STORY

Process Questions

1. How does Bill's story of change compare to your own? _____

   _____

   _____

   _____

   _____

2. Bill discusses ways he practices being a good listener. Describe a time when you were not a good listener. List some ways you could have done things differently to improve your listening. _____

   _____

   _____

   _____

   _____

   _____

   _____

   _____

3. Describe how you feel about talking to other men about your need to control others. _____

   _____

   _____

   _____

   _____

   _____

   _____

   _____

Chapter 10

PARENTING: HOW TO RELATE TO YOUR CHILDREN

I n this last chapter of the book, we would like to take the emphasis off of your relationship with your partner and focus on your interaction with your children. If you currently do not have children, this chapter is still important because you never know if you may have a child in the future or marry someone with children. Whatever your plan or current situation is, the impact of your behaviors and attitudes on a child is worth examining.

In our experience working with groups, we have found that many group members are unsure about how their behavior effects their children. The truth is: They are watching you. Think of your children as sponges, soaking up your words, actions, and attitudes. They are observing you and are constantly learning about the world around them. For children, parents are their prime source for learning about how to be a human being. Your children are learning what it means to be a man, a husband, a father, a wife, a mother, a woman. They are learning how to treat others and how others should be treated by watching your interactions with them and your partner. If you were wondering how they are impacted by your behavior remember: They are watching.

We consider this chapter to be very important. The impact of domestic violence on your children often gets ignored as your partner seeks help and as you seek help and complain about the consequences of your behavior. The exercises in this chapter will explore your parenting style and discuss ways of changing that style as you see fit. Throughout your total experience of being a parent, we encourage you to continuously ask yourself the question, "What are they learning from me today?" Remember: They are watching and learning.

Exercise 10.1
Parenting

The Impact of Domestic Violence on Children

Purpose: Throughout this book, we have explored the impact of violence on you and your partner. We felt that a special section should be given to the impact of domestic violence on children. Many group members, when first discussing this topic, have said that they believe that their kids don't know about the problems in the marital relationship because the kids don't "see" the violence. Many men report going to great lengths to "protect" their kids from being exposed to the violence in the house. Statements such as "we only fight when the kids are asleep" or "we take the kids to Grandma's house if things get rough" are evidence of how parents try to protect their children from the abuse between them. Unfortunately, research and personal experience in group has shown us that children are impacted (Jaffe, Wolfe, & Wilson, 1990). This exercise explores the effect of controlling behaviors on your children (any and all behaviors discussed in Chapter 2, Exercise 2.2: Personal Continuum of Controlling Behaviors).

Materials: The Impact of Domestic Violence on Children Fact Sheet; Impact Questionnaire.

Procedure: Read each item on The Impact of Domestic Violence on Children Fact Sheet. As you read the items, comment on how you have seen these characteristics in your own children. Once again, we encourage you to be as honest as possible. Although you may experience feelings of shame and embarrassment, the only way you can help your children is to be accountable for your behaviors and change the controlling and abusive patterns in your life. Answer the Impact Questionnaire. Bring the worksheets to group and process your answers and resulting feelings with the group.

EXERCISE 10.1: THE IMPACT OF DOMESTIC VIOLENCE ON CHILDREN FACT SHEET

1. **Increased feelings of fear** as evidenced by clinging behavior, crying spells, nightmares, etc.

   Comments and Evidence: _____

   _____

   _____

   _____

2. **Poor social skills.**

   Comments and Evidence: _____

   _____

   _____

   _____

3. **Easily distracted or hypervigilant.** This causes problems in school and other structured activities.

   Comments and Evidence: _____

   _____

   _____

   _____

4. **More prone to delinquency, sexual acting out, substance abuse problems, and impulse control problems.**

   Comments and Evidence: _____

   _____

   _____

   _____

5. Despite parents' efforts to keep violence a "secret," the **children will sense an atmosphere of fear in the house.**

   Comments and Evidence: _____

   _____

   _____

   _____

6. **Learn that violence is the way to problem solve,** as evidenced by fights at school, at home, or with friends.

   Comments and Evidence: _____

   _____

   _____

   _____

7. *Learn gender roles from parent interaction.* For example, boys learn that women are to be controlled and girls learn it is normal to be victimized and abused. The real question here is, "Your children are watching you. What are they learning?"

   Comments and Evidence: _____

   _____

   _____

   _____

8. **Either want to stay home all the time or want to be away from home as much as possible.** The key here is the fear of the violence drives both strategies. Some children feel like their presence decreases the chance of violence. They are the protectors. Others have experienced violence first hand, feel helpless to stop it, and want to escape to terror at home.

   Comments and Evidence: _____

   _____

   _____

   _____

EXERCISE 10.1: THE IMPACT OF DOMESTIC VIOLENCE ON CHILDREN

Impact Questionnaire

1. Have you ever yelled at your partner in front of your children? If so, how was the argument resolved? Did the children see this resolution?

   _____

   _____

   _____

   _____

   _____

   _____

   _____

2. Have you ever called your partner a name in front of your children?

   _____

3. Have you ever physically abused your partner in front of your children? If so, how do you feel it has impacted them? _____

   _____

   _____

   _____

   _____

   _____

   _____

   _____

4. Discuss a time when you were abusive, but waited until the children went to sleep to act out on your partner. Why did you wait until they went to sleep? Did your plan work?_____

_____

_____

_____

_____

_____

_____

_____

_____

5. Have you ever threatened your partner with "taking away the children"? How does this threat impact the children?_____

_____

_____

_____

_____

_____

_____

_____

_____

_____

You may have noticed that the questions make it seem like there is no right way to fight. If you are abusive in front of the children, then they are directly harmed by the exposure to the abuse. If you try to "shield" them by sending them away or waiting until they go to sleep, then they will sense the tension in the house and will still be afraid of what is going on in the house. Your feelings are on target. The main point here is that abuse and control, whether experienced first hand or indirectly, have a high probability of impacting your children negatively. The problem is not whether you argue in front of your children, but *how* you argue. Abusive and controlling behavior is not acceptable or helpful in any situation, and is hurting not only you and your partner, but also your children. In the space below, use your knowledge of your personal continuum (go back to Chapter 2), your accountability skills (see Chapter 6), and your communication skills (see Chapter 9) to make a plan to repair the damage your behavior may have caused, and at the very least, demonstrate a change for the future. _____

_____

_____

_____

_____

_____

_____

_____

_____

_____

_____

_____

_____

_____

Exercise 10.2
Parenting

Exploring Your Parenting Style

Purpose: The last exercise was designed to make you aware of how your behavior effects your children. Overall, your actions, beliefs, and feelings make up your general parenting style: how you interact with and parent your children. If you don't have children, your attitudes and actions will still be used to generate a decision about having children and what your expectations of your children will be as they grow. Since you were a child yourself once, you have seen parents in action as you watched your own parents struggle. The interaction between past and present experiences make up our total view of how fathers, mothers, and children should behave in relation to each other. In searching for ways to change our parenting styles, we must first examine what has contributed to our current style.

Materials: Your Parenting Style Worksheet.

Procedure: Answer each of the questions on the Parenting Style worksheet. If you currently do not have children, answer the questions as if you did have children. The second copy of the worksheet is for your partner to complete. The partner's copy is to be used as a way to gauge how similar or different your parenting attitudes and experiences are compared to your partner's. It should be your partner's decision whether or not to participate. Using your partnership and communication skills, the open discussion of parenting views can be a bonding experience for you if you remember to value differences of opinion. After you have completed your portion, bring your answers to group and discuss them with the group. Note differences and similarities in parenting styles within your own group.

EXERCISE 10.2: EXPLORING YOUR PARENTING STYLE

Your Parenting Style Worksheet

1. Describe your father as a parent. How did he treat your mom? Your brothers? Your sisters? You? _____

    _____

    _____

    _____

2. What elements of your father's parenting style have you adopted? What elements have you ignored? _____

    _____

    _____

    _____

3. Describe your mother as a parent? How did she treat your father? Your brothers? Your sisters? _____

    _____

    _____

    _____

    You? _____

    _____

    _____

    _____

4. What elements of your mother's parenting style have you adopted? What elements have you ignored?

    _____

    _____

    _____

    _____

    _____

5. How were you disciplined as a child? What did you learn as a child from this discipline? _____

_____

_____

_____

6. How do you discipline your own children? What is your evidence that your form of discipline works? Why did you choose this type of discipline? _____

_____

_____

_____

7. How did your parents show they loved you? _____

_____

_____

_____

8. How do you show your children that you love them? Why did you choose these ways? _____

_____

_____

9. As a child, did you feel that it was okay for parents to make mistakes?

_____

_____

_____

10. As a parent, how do you let your children know it is okay to make mistakes? _____

_____

_____

_____

EXERCISE 10.2: EXPLORING YOUR PARENTING STYLE

Partner's Parenting Style Worksheet

1. Describe your father as a parent. How did he treat your mom? Your brothers? Your sisters? You? _____

   _____

   _____

   _____

2. What elements of your father's parenting style have you adopted? What elements have you ignored? _____

   _____

   _____

   _____

3. Describe your mother as a parent? How did she treat your father? Your brothers? Your sisters? _____

   _____

   _____

   _____

   You? _____

   _____

   _____

   _____

4. What elements of your mother's parenting style have you adopted? What elements have you ignored?

   _____

   _____

   _____

   _____

   _____

5. How were you disciplined as a child? What did you learn as a child from this discipline?_____

_____

_____

_____

6. How do you discipline your own children? What is your evidence that your form of discipline works? Why did you choose this type of discipline?_____

_____

_____

_____

7. How did your parents show they loved you?_____

_____

_____

_____

8. How do you show your children that you love them? Why did you choose these ways?_____

_____

_____

9. As a child, did you feel that it was okay for parents to make mistakes?

_____

_____

_____

10. As a parent, how do you let your children know it is okay to make mistakes?_____

_____

_____

_____

Exercise 10.3
Parenting

Encouragement vs. Discouragement

Purpose: According to Dreikurs and Cassel (1974), "A child needs encouragement like a plant needs sun and water" (p. 49). If encouragement is the sun and water, discouragement can be seen as cutting the roots. While interacting with your child in an encouraging way will foster self-esteem and courage, communicating with your child in a discouraging manner will hamper growth and has a high probability of adding to the fear, anger, and isolation that has already been established by the atmosphere of tension created by your abusive and controlling behaviors. This exercise is designed to aid you in developing an encouraging relationship with your child. The difference among praise, encouragement, and discouragement will be explored.

Materials: Praise, Encouragement, and Discouragement sheet with questions.

Procedure: Read over the Praise, Encouragement, and Discouragement sheet. Notice the differences among the three forms of interaction. While most people can easily see the difference between discouragement and encouragement, most people have a difficulty recognizing the difference between praise and encouragement. While praise only rewards perfection, encouragement recognizes the effort and success in every action. While praise focuses on comparing the child to others or an imaginary perfection, encouragement relates to how the child has worked to achieve whatever result was achieved: positive or negative. Praise tends to foster competition and a constant need for approval, where encouragement fosters cooperation and the satisfaction received from contributing to the project and doing one's best. As you look over the examples, try to imagine how your children would respond to the different types of interactions.

PRAISE, ENCOURAGEMENT, AND DISCOURAGEMENT

Praise	Encouragement	Discouragement
1. You cleaned up your room just like I told you to!	You really worked hard at cleaning up your room!	You left a sock out. I hope you do better next time.
2. You got an "A!" That's my girl!	I can tell you are very proud of your grade!	You may have made an "A" in Science, but what about Math?
3. You make me happy when you tell the truth.	It was brave of you to tell the truth even though you knew you would be grounded.	I can't believe you disobeyed me! I don't want to hear another word!
4. You don't need my help. You're the smartest one in class!	I am confident you will do your best.	Here, just let me do it for you.
5. I like you a lot better when you are wearing your smile!	You look very happy today. Would you tell me about your day?	It's nice that one of us had an easy day! (Sarcastic)
6. You're doing great! Growing up just like your old man!	You're looking forward to going to high school and trying out all the cool new opportunities.	All teenagers are the same. They think they know everything. I was your age too, I didn't know crap and neither do you!

EXERCISE 10.3: ENCOURAGEMENT
VS. DISCOURAGEMENT

Processing Questions

1. Your child has just come home and has made a "B" on a math exam. The child seems very excited. Demonstrate how you would respond below:

   Praise:_____

   _____

   Encouragement:_____

   _____

   Discouragement:_____

   _____

2. In your opinion, how do you feel you interact with your child? List some examples to support your position._____

   _____

   _____

   _____

   _____

   _____

3. This exercise can also be applied to your partner. Much like we explored in the Trust Tube exercise, if you are not actively being encouraging in your relationship, then you are being discouraging. Discuss ways you are encouraging or can be encouraging in your relationship.

   _____

   _____

   _____

   _____

   _____

Exercise 10.4
Parenting

Punishment vs. Discipline

Purpose: In the last exercise, we learned the difference between helpful and not-so-helpful ways of interacting with your children on a daily basis. All parents know that there will be times when a child will "act up" or "break the rules of the house." There are many ways of handling problems when they occur. This exercise explores two general categories: punishment and discipline. Each category will be explored by characteristics developed by battering groups and a number of helpful resources (Nelsen, Lott, & Glenn, 1993; Popkin, 1990). You will have the opportunity to explore your own experiences and consider which method works best for you and your family.

Often, we adopt the method that was used by our parents or a method that is the mirror image of how we were treated (see Exercise 10.2: Exploring Parenting Style). Whatever the reason may be, too many times we adopt strategies without thinking them out in detail. The purpose of this exercise is to look at all options so each person can make an informed choice.

Materials: Punishment vs. Discipline Comparison and Questions

Procedure: Read over the Punishment vs. Discipline Comparison sheet. Compare the characteristics of each method to the answer you reported on questions #5 and #6 of the Exploring Your Parenting Style worksheet. Consider each method as if you were a new parent, trying to decide how you were going to treat your child. Answer each of the process questions as openly as possible. Bring your answers to group and discuss your opinions with your group. After you have discussed the issues, you may want to explore the exercise with your partner and listen to what she thinks about the different methods.

PUNISHMENT VS. DISCIPLINE

Punishment	*Discipline*
1. Means "inflict pain."	1. Means "to instruct."
2. Uses force, violence and intimidation.	2. Uses respect and firm limits.
3. Is humiliating to the child; is discouraging	3. Promotes self-respect; is encouraging.
4. Is inconsistent and largely depends on who is doing the punishing.	4. Is consistent within the child.
5. Expectations of the child are often vague: "Do what I say."	5. Expectations are clearly spelled out before problems start.
6. Parent is responsible for creating and giving the punishment: "You messed up, I'm going to have to ground you."	6. Child is responsible for consequences through a verbalized choice: "If you choose to break curfew, then you also choose to stay home on Friday night."
7. Consequences are not related to the incident: "You broke a glass so you get a spanking."	7. Consequences are related to the incident: "You broke a glass, so you can clean it up.
8. Emphasizes what *not* to do.	8. Emphasizes what to do.
9. Consequences do not change as child matures. If you spank your two-year-old, you will probably use the same technique with your nine-year-old.	9. Consequences change as child matures.
10. Effects are short-term and cannot be generalized to other situations.	10. Effects are long-term and can be generalized to other situations.
11. Only works when you (the punisher) are around.	11. Choice comes from the child, so discipline works in your absence.
12. Instills guilt.	12. Instills accountability.
13. Teaches that anger and aggression are good ways of handling conflict.	13. Teaches that making choices are a good way of avoiding conflict.

EXERCISE 10.4: PUNISHMENT VS. DISCIPLINE

Processing Questions

1. As you compared your way of disciplining your children to the two categories, which of the two categories best matches your parenting style?

    _____

2. What are some of your personal reasons for not using the other approach? _____

    _____

    _____

    _____

    _____

3. Many parents use punishment, especially spanking, as a means to control their children. What is your opinion about spanking? What do you think it teaches children? List examples to support your views._____

    _____

    _____

    _____

    _____

4. Many people do not use "discipline" because they feel it is too permissive. What do you think? _____

    _____

    _____

    _____

    _____

    _____

5. In many, families "the punisher" is the father. This is seen when the mother says, "Wait until your father gets home!" How does this impact your relationship with your children? How do you feel about that impact? _____

_____

_____

_____

_____

_____

6. Experts believe that punishment comes from the parents' need for power and control, while discipline comes from mutual respect. In your quest to become less controlling, what are some steps you can take to use more discipline-like strategies in your home? _____

_____

_____

_____

_____

_____

7. List at least three questions you have about the difference between punishment and discipline. Bring them to group and discuss them with other members. _____

_____

_____

_____

_____

_____

Exercise 10.5
Parenting

Zack's Story: Balancing Work and Family

When I first started this group, I was real confused. I thought my life was a mess, I was a failure, and the real kicker was that I had no idea how to fix it! I'm 38 years old and for the last eighteen years I have been working twelve-hour swing shifts at the factory. I hated my work. I mean, I liked the money but the work was hard and boring and the hours sucked. Anyway, the whole reason why I worked so hard was so I could provide for my family. I started working there as soon as Sharon got pregnant. Three years later we had another kid, so that meant we needed more money. I took overtime every chance I got because I thought we needed the money. I thought I was doing what I was supposed to be doing as the man, as the husband, and as a father.

The problem was that four years ago my marriage hit the rocks. I was totally blind-sided. Here I was, slaving away for my family and my family was leaving! What was it all for? I became abusive to Sharon to get her to stay. What was I thinking? She didn't stay because she loved me. She stayed because she was scared of what I might do.

I now realize that even though I thought I was working for my family, I never asked them what they needed. I missed a lot of my kids' growing up because I was working. The money's been forgotten and can be replaced, but I'll never be able to replace what I've missed. I can't believe all they wanted was some of my time. It's a family joke now. My oldest son will say, "Dad, I don't need a new pair of shoes this week. Why don't you come play some hoops with me?" I wonder how many times he thought that while he was growing up, but I wasn't around to hear it.

I still believe part of being a good parent is providing for your family, but I now know it goes way beyond money. To be a real parent, you have to provide time. I never would have believed it four years ago, but it's saved my family and Lord knows I like not working as much!

EXERCISE 10.5: ZACK'S STORY

Process Questions

1. Before Zack "changed," what did he believe was his role as a parent? How did his view change? Why did it change? _____

   _____

   _____

   _____

   _____

2. How does Zack's experience as a parent compare to your own? _____

   _____

   _____

   _____

   _____

3. What is your role as a parent? How did you get this role? Zack thought he was fulfilling his role, but he actually wasn't giving the family what they needed. He was caught off guard because he was functioning out of his own expectations and did not consult with his family. What steps can you take to consider the needs of your family when determining what your role will be as a parent? _____

   _____

   _____

   _____

   _____

   _____

   _____

   _____

TIPS FOR BALANCING WORK AND FAMILY

The following tips have been compiled through our work with battering groups and from a book on the subject by Levine and Pittinsky (1997).

1. Talk to your family about expectations and time commitments needed from each member.

2. Realize that money will not solve your problems. It may help you feel good for awhile, but it cannot provide a parental substitute. Work on a budget together.

3. Make use of the telephone to connect with your family when you're at work. It demonstrates that you are thinking about them.

4. Find at least one consistent time a week that is set aside for each child. Put it down on your schedule and treat it like it is the most important assignment in the world. Your job (as a parent) depends on it! After you have this down, try once a day.

5. Talk to them like you know what they are up to. Instead of saying "How was your day?", ask "How did your biology project go?" It shows that you are interested and that you have been paying attention.

6. When you get home, you probably want to unwind. Find something relaxing that you can do with the whole family. One group member took all the money he worked extra hours for and spent it on a hot tub. Every evening when he comes home, everyone gets in the hot tub and relaxes. He said it was the best investment he ever made.

7. Develop a going home ritual to relieve work stress. Your kids are not the proper outlet for your work stress. Listen to the radio, go work out before going home, anything to help you make the transition so you will not treat those at home like you would like to treat those at work.

8. Most importantly—kiss them, hug them, and show them that you love them with your time!

CONCLUSION

As you end the journey through this workbook, we would like you to take a moment to look back at the enormous amount of work you have completed. As you flip back over the pages, you will see the evidence of an exploration of yourself that was difficult at times. You will see evidence of moments that you were honest with yourself, and you will see writing where you lied to yourself by not putting down all you knew about yourself. You will remember points of learning and points of disappointment, anger, and resentment. No matter what you find when you look back, we want you to realize it took a lot of work on your part.

Making the change into a less controlling, less abusive individual takes time and courage. Most of all, change is a process. You are not finished because you completed this workbook or your group time. Maintaining your new skills means constant practice in good times and trying times. It means remembering "You cannot control others. You can only control yourself" and using it in your daily life; some of the exercises in this workbook will have to be revisited numerous times before you feel like it is second nature.

Even though change may be difficult, we hope you have seen its advantages. Trying to cooperate with your partner instead of controlling her will make your life less stressful. As you have learned, feeling like you have to be in control of everything and everyone can eat you alive. Although you may "feel like a man" for carrying the world on your shoulders, wouldn't it be nice if you had someone to help you carry the world? Engaging in a partnership and listening to your partner allows you the freedom to relax and share the burdens of life.

We ask that you continue to explore your feelings and attitudes toward the situations and people in your life. Many people who finish group say, "You'll never see me again. I will never hit her again." To them, and to you, we say, we hope you are never arrested again for domestic violence. If you haven't been arrested, we hope that you never feel scared enough about your behavior that you feel like you have to enter a program again. We hope your partners never have to endure abuse again. We hope your children grow up in a happy home where differences of opinion are honored and moms and dads treat each other with respect. We also know that saying it will not make it happen. You, and only you, must commit yourself to a life without violence.

Throughout this book you have been given the opportunity to pick up some new tools for your toolbox. We do not know which ones you have chosen. If you are reading this and you are saying to yourself that you have learned nothing, then you have chosen nothing. It is impossible to believe that you will think, feel, or behave any differently when you are using the same tools of control and abuse. However, if you believe you have some new tools, we encourage you to use them. Like any other tool, they are only as good as the person using them, so use them well.

Before we leave, there is one last exercise and one last sheet of information. You are invited to return to the book as often as you like for "booster shots" of information. Good luck!

WRITE YOUR OWN STORY

Throughout this book, you have read stories of men who have gone through a process similar to yours. Pick a topic and write your own story, demonstrating how you feel in the present. You may want to read your story to your group and/or to your partner.

_____

_____

_____

_____

_____

_____

_____

_____

_____

_____

_____

_____

_____

_____

_____

_____

POEM OF HOPE FOR CHANGE

As a closing tradition, each person who completes the Battering Intervention Program has been given the opportunity to speak to the group about personal reflections on the group process. Usually members will briefly discuss what they have learned, changes they have made, and changes that still need to be made. Members also take the opportunity to say good-bye and good luck to their support structure: the group. When it came time for a certain member to say good-bye, he did something very unique. He stood up in front of the group, took a deep breath, and expressed to us his growth in the most sincere way he knew: a poem he had written for his graduation day. The poem is printed here as a reminder to those of you who have the courage to change. There is hope.

Graduation
March 18, 1997

When faced with anger it's better to turn and walk from the danger.
Talk to a friend instead of a stranger.
So if the love is gone and there is no doubt
and your anger grows and you begin to shout
turn around and just walk out.

For if you stay you might have to pay,
and it's easier to discuss another day.
For every time she hurt or cried, I felt deep down our love had died.
For now I see the problems we brought
could have been avoided if we wouldn't have fought.
However, in life we'll be faced with decisions
and it would mean a lot to pay attention
or the least you could do is sit and listen.

When you're feeling scared or when in doubt
or feeling hurt and all alone,
it sometimes helps to let your feelings be known.
I believe she feels the same.
Just remember she's not to blame.
So do your best and love all you can.
Be supportive and lend a hand.
It will make you feel like a better man.
Just remember: Don't ever raise your hand.

REFERENCES

Bathrick, D., Carlin, K., Kaufman, G., & Vodde, R. (1987). *Men stopping violence: A program for change*. Atlanta, GA: Men Stopping Violence, Inc.

Brooks, G. R. (1995). *The centerfold syndrome*. San Francisco: Jossey-Bass.

Bureau of Justice. (1994). *Violence against women*. Washington, DC: U.S. Department of Justice.

Bureau of Justice. (1996). *National crime victimization survey*. Washington, DC: U.S. Department of Justice.

Covey, S. (1990). *The seven habits of highly effective people*. New York: Fireside.

Dreikurs, R., & Cassel, P. (1974). *Discipline without tears*. New York: Hawthorn.

Federal Bureau of Investigation. (1996). *Uniform crime statistics*. Washington, DC: Author.

Jaffe, P. G., Wolfe, D. A., & Wilson, S. K. (1990). *Children of battered women*. Newbury Park, CA: Sage.

Levine, J. A., & Pittinsky, T. L. (1997). *Working fathers: New strategies for balancing work and family*. New York: Addison-Wesley.

Nelsen, J., Lott, L., & Glenn, H. S. (1993). *Positive discipline A-Z*. Rocklin, CA: Prima.

Peck, M. S. (1993). *Further along the road less traveled*. New York: Simon & Schuster.

Pence, E., & Paymar, M. (1993). *Education groups for men who batter: The Duluth model*. New York: Springer.

Popkin, M. H. (1990). *Active parenting of teens: Parent's guide*. Atlanta, GA: Active Parenting, Inc.

Tannen, D. (1990). *You just don't understand*. New York: Ballantine.

Trotzer, J. P. (1997). *Problem solving group counseling*. A presentation to the Association for Specialists in Group Work, Athens, GA.

Zilbergeld, B. (1992). *The new male sexuality*. New York: Bantam.

INDEX

About the Authors

Kevin A. Fall, Ph.D., is an Assistant Professor at Loyola University—New Orleans. He has been active as a group counselor in hospital, agency, and private practice settings. He earned his Ph.D. from the University of North Texas and holds credentials as a Nationally Certified Counselor and is a Licensed Professional Counselor in both Texas and Louisiana.

Fall's counseling interests include adolescent issues, group counseling, domestic violence intervention, and the application of Adlerian theory. He is the co-author of Group Counseling: Concepts and Procedures, with Berg and Landreth. He was employed as a co-director of the battering intervention program at Denton County Friends of the Family and has presented at the national, state, and local levels on the topic of group treatment for domestic violence offenders. In addition to counselor education, Fall maintains a private practice that focuses on adolescents and groups. He also currently works with schools to facilitate unique group opportunities for pre-adolescent and adolescent males.

Shareen Howard, M.S., is the director of the Battering Intervention and Prevention Program (BIPP) at Denton County Friends of the Family in Denton, Texas. She received her Master's degree in Counseling and Development from Texas Women's University. She is also a Licensed Professional Counselor in Texas. She has worked extensively with the survivors and perpetrators of domestic violence and firmly believes that intervention is necessary at all levels in order to end domestic violence.

June E. Ford, LMSW, M.S.S.W., is the executive director of an assisted living community in Denton, Texas. She earned her B.S.W. at Texas Women's University and her M.S.S.W. from the University of Texas at Arlington. She has worked as a battering intervention group facilitator of both men's and women's groups and has served as co-director of the Battering Intervention and Prevention Program at Denton County Friends of the Family. She continues to volunteer her services as a BIPP group leader.